PAST LIFE HEALING

PAST LIFE HEALING

At Peace with Today
by Visiting Yesterday

JUDY SHARP
Winner of the national Spiritual Writing Competition

Judy Sharp © 2022

All rights reserved
in accordance with the Copyright, Designs and Patents Act 1988.

No parts of this publication may be reproduced, stored in a retrieval system, or transmitted in any form or by any means whatsoever without the prior permission of the publisher.

A record of this publication is available from the British Library.

ISBN 978-1-910027-52-3

Typesetting by Wordzworth Ltd
www.wordzworth.com

Cover design by Titanium Design Ltd
www.titaniumdesign.co.uk

Cover images by courtesy of Elizabeth Villalta
and Sixteen Miles Out

Published by Local Legend
www.local-legend.co.uk

Dedicated to all those who have taught me so much
over the years and especially to all the therapy clients
who have allowed me to support them on their healing journeys.

Acknowledgements

I am deeply grateful for the love and support of my soulmate, the Genie, across lifetimes, and to Local Legend for their support and encouragement.

Disclaimer

All the personal names of clients and any other identifiers used in this book have been changed to protect their privacy.

www.local-legend.co.uk

About the Author

Judy's spiritual journey started when she moved to Portugal after successful corporate careers in the UK and Gibraltar. Her mind was opening to the concept of complementary therapies and to spirituality, and the urgent need to resolve her own chronic claustrophobia led her to a hypnotherapist who used regression to find the root cause, a life in ancient Egypt.

"In just one session," she says, "the claustrophobia was gone and I was hooked." So began her second professional career, training in psychotherapy and hypnotherapy, using past life regression for healing.

More than twenty-five years later, in her native England, she has helped countless clients to trace back the underlying root causes of issues ranging from fear of heights or of flying to lost libido or stubborn weight gain. By discovering past life trauma, many such issues can be resolved at source, allowing clients to move on peacefully with their current lives.

Judy's website is www.effective-hypnotherapy.co.uk

Contents

Foreword		1
Introduction		3
Chapter 1	Fears and Phobias	9
Chapter 2	My Life, My Work	21
Chapter 3	Food Issues and Weight Loss	33
Chapter 4	Social History	45
Chapter 5	Defending My People	59
Chapter 6	Reincarnation, the Concept and Early Research	73
Chapter 7	Slavery	85
Chapter 8	Wives and Husbands	97
Chapter 9	Health of Body and Mind	111
Chapter 10	Lives Cut Short or Wasted	121
Chapter 11	Modern Research	133
Chapter 12	Gifts Carried Forward	145
Chapter 13	History as It Happened	155
Chapter 14	Physical Issues	167
Chapter 15	Money and Sex	177
Chapter 16	The Spiritual	191
Postscript		201

Foreword

My own exploration of reincarnation has tended to focus on evidential cases where, for example, an individual's claim to have lived a previous life is dramatically confirmed when his or her memories are verified as real. In exceptional cases, they are even reunited with that past life family. Reports of meticulously researched reincarnation cases are to be found at the University of Virginia, Charlottesville, USA, and several other academic centres around the world.

As a therapist, Judy Sharp's approach to the subject is very different but equally valid. Those who seek her help are not looking for evidence of a previous life and nor is she. It is her patients' problems or issues in this life that need resolving. In the process, her therapeutic techniques frequently involve her clients realising that the root causes can be traced back to events or relationships in a previous incarnation.

It might sound unbelievable, but the rich past life tapestry that often emerges is fascinating, sometimes heartrending and frequently reads like the plot of a bestselling novel. But most important of all is that it can be highly effective in helping them understand and overcome the issues that have led them to her door.

Past Life Healing is a very well written casebook study that explores important questions about the power of the mind, our spiritual development across many lives and the unrecognised importance of soul memory in that exciting and often challenging journey. In doing so, it encourages us to benefit from looking at our current life as part of a much greater picture.

Judy Sharp concludes with these wise words: "It is so important not to judge anyone because we cannot know what journey their soul is on."

Roy Stemman

Author of *One Soul: Many Lives* (Ulysses Press, 2005) and
The Big Book of Reincarnation (Hierophant Publishing, 2012)

Introduction

The young architect picked up rolls of plans and set off to meet his client, the new regional governor and a favourite of the Pharaoh. When he arrived, waiting for him with the governor was the High Priest, who had found out about the secret lessons the architect had been giving, sharing the wisdom and knowledge of the ancients.

They toured the sprawling house and the governor asked the architect to check the dimensions of an underground storage area. Once he was inside, slaves pushed a large slab across the entrance, shutting him in and leaving him there to die. He paid the ultimate price for defying the High Priest.

I was that architect and his traumatic death in ancient Egypt was the cause of my claustrophobia in this lifetime. Finding him and healing him not only cured my phobia, it set me on my path as a past life regression therapist.

Funny old things, past lives. One of them may just pop up out of the blue when you least expect it, a flashback to another place and time. And if you go looking for one, you never quite know what you are going to find, perhaps even two or three at once. But the lovely thing is, however traumatic they may appear to be at first, they are invariably informative, insightful and powerful healing tools for resolving issues in this life.

Past life regression work was amazingly effective in healing my own claustrophobia. Previously, there was no way I could go into an enclosed space, especially underground, if there was no window or means of escape. It was sorted after just one session, so it was an obvious move for me to add this specialist practice into my psychotherapy training.

When I started, there was little knowledge of the subject and it was certainly not accepted as openly as it is now. Indeed, it was seen as a bit of a novelty, a party trick: "Go on, do me!" And the usual objections were that the client was just making it all up or had read it in a book somewhere.

Why on Earth would someone instantly make up a story of being a young boy in the Middle Ages whose father has left home to find work because the crops have failed and there is no food? The ten year-old boy has to look after his mother and her new-born baby so, knowing there are potatoes in the lord of the manor's barn, he creeps in and steals a few to feed his family. But he's caught and hanged from a tree in front of his parents' house, his mother forced to watch. No wonder my client, in this lifetime, could not bear to wear a tie or even have a scarf around his neck.

Well, do I then feed suggestions to the client? When we start a past life journey, with the intention of healing, I have no idea which life the client is going to find or which character is going to appear. It is I who has to keep up with them, not the other way round! The character from the past sets the pace and provides the information as I ask open-ended questions.

So is my client picking up on an archetype, such as the warrior or the story-teller, the victim or the queen? The amount of detail provided makes this very unlikely and moreover, it has been said, "You can't fake emotions when in a state of relaxation." It is quite something to see tears streaming down someone's face when the past life character is experiencing grief, or their face wincing in pain with what the character is going through.

Not everyone believes in past lives of course and there are those who say that people in a deep state of relaxation may be tapping

INTRODUCTION

into 'the collective unconscious'. This term was coined by the father of psychoanalysis, Carl Jung (1875 – 1961), to describe that part of the deep unconscious mind that is not personal to an individual but rather is shared by all of humankind. This is responsible for deep-rooted beliefs and instincts, a vast reservoir of shared ancestral experiences, knowledge and imagery. In our normal everyday lives we are unaware of this, like one of those computer programs that operate quietly in the background, just doing their thing. Then, in certain situations, instinct kicks in and something is triggered.

A modern spiritual analogy of this is the Akashic Records, said to hold all the information of the entire universe. The so-called 'Sleeping Prophet', Edgar Cayce (1877 – 1945), was a salesman who discovered the amazing gift of being able, when in a deep state of relaxation, to tell people about their past lives and, perhaps more importantly, diagnose strangers' illnesses and prescribe natural remedies to cure their conditions. He gave thousands of such readings in his lifetime[1]. Was he accessing those Akashic Records?

Certainly, when someone is in an induced deep state of relaxation they are in an altered state of consciousness. That's the whole point, to get the conscious and rational mind out of the way, the part that filters thoughts and images with, "Yes, but I'm a man and I couldn't possibly have been a woman in a past life" or "Yes, but I've never been to India." Perhaps past life accounts are indeed tapping into that vast collective unconscious… yet how does this account for the highly personal details that so often emerge, the minutiae of everyday life, a character telling me not only what they are seeing and hearing but also what they feel and smell around them?

---

[1] See the Edgar Cayce Association for Research and Enlightenment (https://edgarcayce.org)

There does seem to be evidence that certain basic fears and phobias have their roots in the dim and distant past of humankind. Fear of the dark or of fire, for example, could well have been learned by our ancestors for their own safety and survival with future generations inheriting those same fears. René Garcia looks at these associations in his *Neurobiology of Fear and Specific Phobias*.[2]

It is virtually impossible, of course, to discuss reincarnation without getting into spirituality and debates about the concepts of life after death or life between lives. There are those who say that there is nothing other than a physical body and, when we die, that's the end of us. For me, this seems a bit wasteful in soul terms and I prefer a recycling approach. My own experiences and those of my clients, along with the research I have done, have all led me to a belief in reincarnation and before doing any regression work with a client I explain in clear terms what is involved. Only if they are comfortable with the process do we go ahead.

The clients whose stories I share here ranged from open-minded sceptics to those eager for the experience. But the bottom line is that, in all cases, the journeys proved effective in their healing.

In this book I offer information about the concept of reincarnation across history and across different cultures and religions, as well as details of early and more modern research into the whole field. Illustrating all of this are lots of real-life stories from my own client files, demonstrating the wide range of issues that have been successfully resolved using regression. These clients are normal, everyday people who did not want more prescription drugs, to try the latest diet or to give up hope completely.

They are ordinary people having extraordinary experiences and, along the way, finding who they really are and getting better.

---

[2] See http://learnmem.cshlp.org/site/misc/terms.xhtml (2017)

INTRODUCTION

How does it work?

You will read, in the life stories, accounts of the client going through a doorway to find a past life and then of me moving the past life character forward in that lifetime.

Once a client is deeply relaxed, I use a visualisation technique to put them at one end of a corridor with doors down either side. Each door represents a past life and they will, I suggest to them, be drawn to one door in particular that will lead to the past life most relevant to the work we are doing. When the past life character has introduced themself, I ask them to move forward – it's usually forward but it can be backwards too – to the next important event in that life. So when you read something like, "I next met Doris five years later" or "Moving on, Fred was still making a fortune", this is the process, moving them on to the next key point in that lifetime.

One question I am often asked is whether everyone relaxes easily and finds an appropriate door. No, not everyone does that. Around five percent of people overall do not go into that nice, deep state of relaxation. For some it will be stress, anxiety or fear that holds them back. For others, it is their perceived loss of control.

Of those who do allow themselves to relax fully, there are few who do not find the door. One lady I worked with, for example, found a spiral staircase leading down instead. I encouraged her to go down and see what she would find. There, she reported that members of her family who had died over the years were waiting for her, including a sister who had only passed in the last month. It was not a past life, but it was exactly what the client needed at that time: reassurance, closure and that overwhelming sense of unconditional love that only comes from 'the other side'.

I take my cue from the unconscious, or higher self, of the client because it always knows what the client needs and will take advantage of the opportunity to enable healing to take place at that deep soul level.

A number of other authors' books will be referred to and these would make a good starting point if you wish to do your own research. They each come at the subject in their own way, as a researcher, as a therapist or simply telling a personal story. Some of them have an emphasis on historical accuracy. It is always fascinating when a client comes up with, for instance, the detailed floorplan of an old house that was absolutely correct for their time but which has changed since, or can provide details of an ancient civilisation that archaeologists had not yet discovered.

For me, it is finding the underlying root cause of an issue that, in this lifetime, is having a negative impact on someone's health or lifestyle that is pre-eminently important. My mantra is, "Find the root cause. Resolve it at source. Move on with your life."

As some of my clients have said, "It's weird, but it works!"

CHAPTER 1

Fears and Phobias

A phobia is an irrational fear of something. There are so many, a complete A to Z from Acrophobia (fear of heights) to Zelophobia (fear of jealousy). There's even Arachibutyrophobia, the fear of being choked by peanut butter when it sticks to the roof of the mouth! Many of these fears are so intense that they affect our health or genuinely hold us back from enjoying life to the full.

I have come to believe that such phobias often have their root cause in a past life and over the years I have helped countless clients overcome an array of them. After all, it was my own claustrophobia that led me some years ago to a hypnotherapist to find a solution – and my healing that led me to do this work.

It had been a good day for the young architect. His biggest project to date, a house for the new provincial governor, was nearing completion and it would certainly make his reputation. A messenger arrived to summon him to meet the governor, a personal favourite of the Pharaoh, and he must not be late so he picked up his rolls of plans and set off, heading west out of town. The Egyptian sun was still searingly hot even in the late afternoon. In a couple of hours the tall, tapered towers on each corner of the new house would stand out against the setting sun, creating an impressive silhouette on the skyline and, the architect smiled at the thought, flattering his client's ego too.

The governor had already arrived on site and was waiting with the High Priest. This seemed a little strange but of course it was the client's privilege to show off their property to whomsoever they chose. As they started to tour the house, the architect noted with pride that the master builders had done their work well, the sacred numbers and geometry of the design creating a pleasing sense of symmetry and grace. Columns and archways had been beautifully carved and the stonework was perfect, although he didn't understand why the builders had left a large stone slab by the entrance to one of the underground storage rooms. He made a mental note to ask.

And it was just there that the governor and the High Priest stopped, asking the architect to check the dimensions of the underground room so they could calculate how many jars it would hold. One of the slaves brought a flaming torch and the architect went down the steps...

When he was at the furthest end, he heard a rumbling and scraping noise, and turned to see the stone slab being pushed across the entrance. Was this some kind of joke? Surely the slaves would move the slab back again and let him out? He ran back to the entrance, shouted and banged on the stone, but to no avail. As the hours passed it became clear that it was no joke and nobody was going to let him out. He had been left there to die. The torch fizzled and spluttered out, leaving him in complete darkness.

The architect stood against one of the smooth walls and slid down slowly until he was sitting on the earthen floor. While his body was still, his mind was racing, his emotions in freefall as conversations played out in his head.

"They'll miss me, they'll come looking for me."

"Who will miss you? How will they know where to start looking? Nobody knows where you are."

"My students will miss me, they're coming to my house tonight. They'll wonder where I am."

Ah, his students! That was it. The High Priest must have found out that he was holding classes, passing on the ancient wisdom, the knowledge of numbers and the secrets of nature herself. Yes, he had already suspected this and had warned the young man before, reminded him in no uncertain terms that the penalty for revealing those secrets was death. But surely he didn't mean it, did he? It seems he did, and how clever to involve the new governor, giving him a hold over the Pharaoh's favourite.

Time passed. How much, it was impossible to tell. Complete silence, complete darkness and the inevitability of death surrounded the young man. Only total exhaustion and fitful sleep brought occasional relief. Alone with his thoughts, he began to ponder the meaning of life – and the process of dying.

"Will I starve or will I suffocate? What will happen to my body when I'm dead? How can my heart be weighed on the scales against the feather of Maat? Will my heart be light enough to allow me safe passage to the afterlife?"

At times, the architect wept in despair as he relived his life and thought of all that he had done and had not done, of those he loved and would never see again. At times, fear overcame him: he clawed at the stone, he pleaded with the gods, he screamed for mercy. And eventually he died, alone there in his tomb, having paid the ultimate price for daring to speak his truth and share the knowledge that could free others from the cruel control of their rulers.

I was that young architect. This was the life I went back to and experienced graphically when I visited a hypnotherapist to resolve my claustrophobia, my debilitating fear of being in enclosed spaces, especially underground. Uncovering that life, reliving those moments and emotions, cured my fear in one session and showed me just how powerful regression can be for healing.

Tony, a former detective in his late fifties, came to see me initially for help with giving up smoking. He had been volunteering as a driver with a local charity since retiring and loved the work, but there was a problem: he just could not drive over high bridges and had to consult a map in order to find routes that avoided them on his journeys. Tony also said that he was petrified of heights and that almost every night, just as he was falling off to sleep, he would jerk awake convinced that he was falling off a cliff. In his eyes, none of this had anything to do with him wanting to give up smoking, though.

I had to convince him that by resolving these other underlying issues, it would be much easier for me to help him kick the habit. Reluctantly, and with obvious cynicism, he agreed that we could do a past life regression session. Actually, Tony was a natural and went into the deep state of relaxation very easily.

We met eighteen year-old Ed who had been a pilot in the Royal Air Force for two months in 1917. Ed told me that he was in a field in Belgium, near the French border. There were ten biplanes there under the command of a French officer.

"He's good," said Ed.

The mission was to drop bombs behind enemy lines near the Somme. Once airborne, Ed said he felt tired and could smell oil and leaking fuel around him. He could see flames and bombs being released from other 'planes. There was a lot of black smoke, a lot of noise and some 'planes were crashing, his own damaged although he made it back to base. He was very sad because only two other pilots had made it back, all the others had been shot down.

"There are no parachutes," he explained. He felt physically sick. Was the mission a success, did the bombs hit their targets? He couldn't tell me.

I next found Ed in a military hospital in Belgium. He had been there a week and a half, he was sick, but it seemed to be a mental breakdown rather than a physical illness. I asked him what he could see around him.

"Nurses," he said, "and lots of rows of beds."

What could he hear?

"Crying."

And what could he smell?

"That smell of washing and cleaning. I can smell people and toilets."

After three weeks in hospital, Ed returned to his unit in Belgium. He said he had to go up but didn't want to, he felt afraid. Three 'planes took off at first light, their mission to scout out enemy positions and defences and then return home. On the return flight there was a lot of enemy fire but he managed to make it back safely.

"There are no parachutes," he repeated. "There's no escape if you're hit and you go up in flames."

Ed's next flight was a bombing mission behind enemy lines, in Belgium near the French border, and it was to be his last. His commentary from the cockpit was dramatic.

"Flames, been hit, spinning… flames, oil, burning… no chance, burn to the ground, that's it, the end is coming… pain, pain, I can't get out, I'm too high to survive…"

Pilot Officer Ed, number 542, died on only his third mission.

In the normal course of events, that life experience alone would have been sufficient to trigger a fear of heights but the phrase that Ed used as he was falling somehow jumped out at me.

"Go back to the first time that you were too high to survive," I told Tony, in his deep state of relaxation.

Back he went again, but this time to the fifteenth century where a soldier called Henry introduced himself. He was twenty-six years-old and he was guarding Warwick Castle for his lord, the Earl of Warwick. Henry told me he was wearing a vest, helmet and mail.

PAST LIFE HEALING

He gave the year as 1460 and said that Henry VI was on the throne of England. According to Henry, the Earl was in London but the armies of York and Essex were fighting around Warwick castle.

"There's fighting everywhere," he commented.

Henry was up on the battlements as the fighting raged below when he was hit by an arrow that penetrated his chainmail. He lost his balance and fell backwards down into the keep, cracking his head as he landed. Just before he died, I asked Henry to review his life.

"It was hard," he said, "looking up there where I was, I couldn't stay up there... so many bodies... I couldn't stop the falling, I lost my balance... pain, pain..."

Those lifetimes – or rather, the ways in which he died – fitted perfectly with Tony's issues in this lifetime. His fear of losing his balance and his fear of heights both resonated with him being high up on the battlements and then falling to his death, and of course of being shot down without a parachute. They also accounted for him having the sensation of falling when he was about to go to sleep. His feedback at the next session was uplifting.

"Wonderful sleep. I was driving my van on Monday over bridges with no worries. No more night jerks before I go to sleep and I'm much calmer at work."

By the way, it seems Henry was pretty accurate historically. He said he worked for the Earl of Warwick and gave the year as 1460. That was the time of the Wars of the Roses when the houses of York (the white rose) and Lancaster (the red rose) were fighting for control of the English throne. The then Earl of Warwick, Richard Neville, was nicknamed 'the kingmaker'. He was very well connected, clearly highly intelligent and a very clever strategist who manipulated would-be kings and arranged marriages in order to further his own ambitions. Indeed, he seized the crown from the Lancastrian Henry VI in 1461, allowing the Yorkist Edward IV to take the throne. But nine years later, in 1470, when Edward stepped out of line, the Earl of Warwick's armies defeated

14

him in battle, seized the throne and restored Henry VI as King of England.

Richard Neville would most certainly have spent a lot of time in London, both at the Royal Court and pursuing his own agendas. He also spent time in France, building alliances and arranging marriages. So it is very likely that armies were fighting around Warwick Castle, which was seen as the second seat of power after London at the time.

Henry had said that it was the armies of York and Essex that were fighting but he also said, "They all look the same." It would only have been the flags and perhaps the colour of vests that would have differentiated the armies. So was it Essex, were the Essex men mercenaries for the House of Lancaster? In any event, a lot of accurate historical boxes were ticked here and Tony, when he came back from that experience, admitted that he knew virtually nothing about English history.

You will be wondering whether he gave up smoking… I followed up with Tony while preparing this book, six years after working with him.

"I haven't had a single sniff of a cigarette since leaving your surgery," he said. "Many thanks!"

The fear of flying is one of the most common phobias and perhaps that's not surprising. It is not exactly natural for human beings to be airborne and we are literally out of our element at thirty thousand feet up.

Under the umbrella of aerophobia there are various specific triggers for the extreme anxiety that people suffer. It may be the take-off and landing, or the fact that they are not in the driving seat, not in control. It may be the thought of turbulence or the idea of being confined in a small space and not being able to get out at will. Add to these the more recent triggers of possible terrorism or antisocial behaviour on the flight and it's not hard to see why people take therapy courses, often run by airlines, or dose themselves up with sleeping pills before a flight.

Mary was a lady in her mid-fifties who had recently become a grandmother for the first time. She was keen to visit her grandson but he was on the other side of the world and Mary had a fear of flying. The trigger was pinpointed clearly – being in a confined space and not being able to get out. Mary told me that, as a child, she had been locked in a wardrobe by her elder brother who had then thrown away the key so that the door had to be broken in order to release her. That alone would be traumatic enough to set up claustrophobia in sensitive people and would certainly need to be resolved.

But I felt there was more.

She had never done any work like this before but her wish to see her grandson was a massive incentive and she was happy to 'give it a go'. In a deep state of relaxation, Mary went back to a past life in India as a man called Amaan. When I met Amaan, he told me he was wearing green silk slippers, silk trousers and a dress-type top. He was in a temple that he described as being a kind of pink colour with gold too, and he was praying to Allah. He said the year was 1650 and that he was forty-one years-old.

Amaan explained that he did not have a home. He lived on the streets with his two children, a daughter aged ten and a son aged two. His wife had recently died of diphtheria, leaving him to bring up the children on his own. In fact, he had been a wealthy man until his wife died but it was his wife's parents who provided the wealth and, when their daughter died, they had turned Amaan and their young grandchildren out of the lovely home they had lived in. Now he was in the temple praying for help and guidance for him and his children.

Nine years later, Amaan was in Calcutta where his daughter, then nineteen, was getting married. It was an arranged marriage but the daughter was very happy, he assured me. The groom came from a good family and Amaan was pleased because it meant his daughter would be wealthy. He was living with his daughter in the large house owned by his future in-laws who were very nice people and who treated him well. I asked about his son and Amaan replied that the boy had died when he was four years-old, also from diphtheria.

When I next met Amaan, he told me there had been an earthquake and he was buried under the house in Calcutta. He was now seventy years-old, very frail and unable to escape from under the rubble. He died there, trapped in an enclosed space that he could not get out of.

Two months after that session, I received an email from Mary.

"Just wanted to let you know how successful my sessions were. I tried a taster flight to Dublin first and then I went for it and flew to Singapore… I am able to fly! It was so nice to visit my grandson and this was made possible because of your help. Many thanks."

There are several interesting points about this lovely past life story. First there's the fact that Mary, a woman, experienced a life as Amaan, a man. It is my understanding that we do indeed have lives as both men and women, for how else could we experience life from both points of view? There is a current theory that those who struggle with accepting the gender they are born with may perhaps be souls who have had several consecutive lives as a man and this is their first lifetime, perhaps ever, as a woman, or vice-versa. There can be no proof of this, of course, but it's an idea that makes sense in the context of reincarnation and the soul's journey.

Amaan's human story here is one of sadness and happiness, as most lives are. It also shows the social structure of that society. He goes from riches to poverty and back to riches during the time we are with him, all based not on his own endeavours but on the wealth of others. He seems to have spent some nine years looking after his children on the streets, which would not have been uncommon. The fact that both his wife and his youngest child died from diphtheria is also a comment on the time. Historical records show there to have been earthquakes in the area of Calcutta (now known as Kolkata) and they would not have to have been massive on the Richter Scale to cause buildings to collapse and trap people. Buildings of that period were not strong enough to withstand tremors, so it is not surprising that the earthquake that trapped Amaan and caused his death in 1679 is not specifically mentioned in official records.

This is an example of historical accuracy being secondary to uncovering the story that resolves the issue of the client in this current lifetime. It would have been interesting, for example, to explore further the social aspects of Amaan's life, how the marriage of his daughter was arranged and whether he had to provide a dowry. But that was not the priority of the session. Given the constraints of time in the here and now and the objective of finding the root cause of Mary's fear of flying, we needed to move Amaan through his life.

Moreover, this story shows how even a 'mild' version of the original trauma in this lifetime can trigger an unconscious memory. For a young child, being locked in a wardrobe would be just as frightening as being trapped under rubble would have been for a grown man. Those fears of being trapped and not being able to escape were locked deep inside Mary, and it was only by tracing the thread all the way back that we were able to find the root cause and heal it at source.

Sandy, a lady in her mid-forties, was a mother to two young boys. She was a very loving, caring mother and was anxious not to pass on to her children a phobia that she had suffered from for as long as she could remember. This was the fear of being ill and, in particular, of vomiting. While Sandy understood that every parent is concerned when their children become ill, she knew that her reactions were far greater than normal. She described it as 'a jolt of panic' deep inside. If one of the boys was nauseous and being sick, she would be terrified. To me, that was a clear indicator of a past life situation.

We found a young girl with bare feet, dirty, wearing just rags. She was on a muddy street, it was noisy, there were people around and some buildings. She said her name was Charlotte, that she was eleven or twelve years-old, and that she lived in a dark room. I asked where her parents were.

"They're somewhere…" she said vaguely, adding that she didn't know if they would come back. I asked if she had brothers and sisters. "Lots, they are all around." Charlotte said she was nearly the eldest and that she and her siblings were all healthy. She explained that they had to find food somehow just to survive, and that's what they did, day by day. She could not tell me what year it was, or what town she was in, or who was on the throne.

A couple of years later, Charlotte told me that everyone was ill, they were being sick and they were dying. There was still no sign of her parents.

"My brothers are dying," she said. "Everyone's being sick, it's everywhere… everyone's out in the street, they're being sick. There are no doctors, everyone's gone. I'm okay but everyone is dying around me and I can't help them." At this point Sandy had tears running down her face in obvious distress.

I next met Charlotte in the countryside, in a white cottage. She told me she was now eighteen or nineteen years-old and that she was much cleaner now. She was with another family, not her own as "They all died or left." She lived in the white cottage and had been in the countryside for a year or two, looking after cows. She thought the year was "sixteen-something" and there was a king on the throne but "They don't like him very much."

Now that Charlotte was safe and away from the plague, I skipped forward a decade and found her married to a man called Jack and a new mother to baby Mary. She told me she was aged about twenty-seven, she was happy with Jack and they lived in a small cottage in the country. Later, at the time of her death, Charlotte was in a bed at her home and her three daughters were with her. But she was not happy about that.

"I don't want them seeing me like this." She felt that she had never been good enough and still carried the guilt that she had not been able to help people when the plague was raging around her and people were dying. "Everyone around me died," she said. "I wasn't good enough to help them."

Returning to the present, Sandy confirmed that she constantly felt that she was 'not good enough', didn't do enough and could not look after her children. Uncovering that past life put the fear of illness and nausea in particular into context, along with the fear and the guilt. But the healing work that was done with Charlotte back in that lifetime healed Sandy too. At the next session, she reported being calmer and much more relaxed with her children and she felt sure that she would be able to cope better if they became ill.

Historically, it is worth noting that Charlotte, coming from a very poor family, only had a rough idea of her own age and could not tell me what year it was or who was on the throne. None of that would have been important to her, all that mattered was scavenging in the streets with her many brothers and sisters to find enough food to survive. The story also showed that Charlotte carried the angst and guilt about not being able to help people as they were dying around her – why should she survive when they didn't? – to her deathbed.

No wonder it left such a massive imprint on the soul, to be carried forward to future lifetimes.

CHAPTER 2

My Life, My Work

Some people come into this world with special gifts. Perhaps their extra-sensory perception is already working so they can see, hear and just know things that most others can't. A shaman I worked with, for instance, told me that when he was a young boy he saw people's auras very clearly, and he even knew when a woman was pregnant before she knew herself. When I asked him how he knew that, he said he saw sparkles around her womb area. After a few embarrassing incidents when he had pointed out to his mother, as children do, which women they were passing in the street were pregnant, she encouraged him to keep such observations to himself.

I wasn't like that, not at all. Spirituality was not on my radar until I reached early middle age by which time I'd had a few adventures and was ready for something new. I'd had a corporate career in PR, marketing and communications in England, and then moved to the south of Spain. Well, it seemed like a good idea and there wasn't even a man involved. I also started my own companies in Gibraltar, which went very well until I had a run-in with a government minister there; I called him a liar and he told me that if I didn't close my companies within a month he would do it for me. Tact and diplomacy were never really my strong points and I paid the price for it, being reduced to nothing.

However, while on the Rock I had been introduced to complementary therapies in the form of a lady called Sylta Kalmbach, a naturopath who had her own centre on the Algarve. I was suffering from too much work, too much stress, too many business lunches and ongoing fatigue. I'm sure many of you have experienced that too. A mutual friend suggested that a session with Sylta would help. I hadn't even realised that I needed help before but I was curious and so made an appointment for the next time she came to Gibraltar.

Complementary treatments had never been in my thinking, I was totally work-focused and very rarely even saw an allopathic doctor. Sylta worked with a pendulum to scan my body, diagnose weaknesses, identify foods that my body could not tolerate and minerals and vitamins that it was lacking. I had never seen a pendulum before, let alone seen one working. Sylta sent me away with a long list of foods and drinks I should not have and a much shorter list of things I could have, along with a long list of vitamins and minerals to be taken at different times of day and evening.

I stuck rigidly to what she prescribed and within weeks had lost two and a half stone in weight, my energy had gone through the roof and it was as though the lights had been switched on again. In hindsight, I was incredibly fortunate that Sylta was my introduction to complementary therapies. If her treatment had not worked so well I would not have taken alternative therapy any further. But it did work, we became friends and I visited her centre a few times.

I closed my companies and found myself kicking my heels in a rented house up the Spanish coast on the Costa del Sol, licking my wounds and feeling very sorry for myself. Destiny stepped in again. Sylta asked me to look after her house and office while she and her husband took a long-overdue holiday. I had nothing else to do so off I went, thinking it would be a three-week working holiday.

The office doubled as the library and I found myself surrounded by books on everything from Ayurveda to Zen, almost none of which I had heard of then. There was a team of therapists working from the centre and they had clearly been briefed to keep an eye on me, which they did. Fortunately this included free sessions in their modalities and I was introduced to Shiatsu, sound healing, Reflexology, Reiki and even rebirthing. It was a completely new way of looking at life and it felt like being dropped into the deep end of a swimming pool – totally submerged but rather wonderful.

Sylta's husband was taken ill and three weeks turned into three months. By that time, I had physically reorganised the office and arranged a programme of talks and workshops for the following year based on all the things I found that interested me in the UK magazines that were lying around. I also read many books while I was there and sometimes would find myself thinking, 'But I know that. How can I already know that, I have never heard of this stuff before?'

This was the start of my spiritual journey, by remembering knowledge that I had accumulated, I have come to believe, long ago in forgotten past lives.

Sylta and her husband were pleased with the way everything was running and asked me to stay on and continue what I'd been doing while they were away. This made me very happy and I stayed for a year as organiser of the business and unofficial PR consultant. At the end of that year I was head-hunted by a local German real estate agent who was looking for an English person who could also speak German and Portuguese (I had taught myself the language). There followed a property business in the Algarve, then freelance work as a marketing/PR consultant and feature writer, work that took me all over Portugal. I was fortunate to visit wonderful places and meet a complete cross-section of people, all the while keeping in close contact with Sylta.

I began to look for a therapy that I could work with alongside my freelance career, and an interest in hypnotherapy was sparked when I met Ron Pittendrigh, a former businessman who had also given up a corporate career and was running a successful private practice. It was his direct approach to hypnotherapy that appealed to me as well as the wide range of issues that could be helped by it. When Ron said that he was going to run a training course at the centre, under the auspices of his old college in London, I jumped at the chance to sign up.

Now, as a freelance writer I was working for a number of regional, national and international magazines and I was well-known in the region. I had just been invited to visit a working salt mine, the only one in the Algarve, and it was a rare opportunity for anyone let alone a foreigner. I was delighted to get the chance of an exclusive. But a week before the visit it suddenly struck me that I hated being in enclosed spaces underground, with no window and no way out! Not wanting to turn down the commission, I turned to Ron.

"You've got a week to sort this out," I told him.

"We've got one day," he replied, smiling gently. "I go on holiday tomorrow for a month."

The session lasted several hours and uncovered one of my 'big lives', as the young architect in ancient Egypt described in Chapter One. At the end of the session, I was exhausted and tissues littered the floor. But the visit to the salt mine passed without incident and I was determined to find out more about past life regression work as a therapy.

Since then I have added many more elements to my professional toolkit, along with the knowledge and practical experience of working in the 'outfield' of hypnotherapy, always with a definite spiritual overlay to my soul-level work with clients.

I have also worked with many teachers across the fields of complementary therapies, spirituality and energy healing, and it was with shaman Tony Samara that I went to Isla del Sol, a small island in Lake Titicaca and 3,500 metres up in the Bolivian Andes. After a ten-day retreat with a small group, I stayed on for three months to live with the indigenous people, documenting their lifestyle. I was learning to live in a completely different way, in harmony with nature, in rhythm with planet Earth and in connection with those higher realms. It is said that Lake Titicaca is the Sacral Chakra of the Earth, and I was there to welcome the dawning of the new millennium, a magical and high-energy time on so many levels.

Life in the Algarve had been good but apparently it was time for me to learn another life lesson... I started a company with an Englishman involved in the international property investment business, finding investors and projects to bring together. The greatest interest was in the German market so I found myself commuting from Portugal, eventually leaving the place that had been home for some twenty years and moving to Berlin, a beautiful place to live. But remember, I had 'something to learn'. The business did not go according to plan and, just under a year later, I found myself selling up and giving away everything. I returned to England with just a dozen small packing cases containing my entire worldly belongings, reduced to nothing for the second time.

When life gives us a kicking and things are just not working out, we need to try and recognise this as an opportunity, nudging us onto a different and better path. It's not easy, though, is it? While I was able to find lodgings with an old friend and get settled, the turbulence of the previous year caught up with me and I slid, not very gracefully, into a deep, black hole of depression. Every now and again the blackout curtains did part, allowing me to see a chink of light that I would move towards; then the curtains would close again. It took almost a year to find my way out of that place, not with prescription drugs but with nature's own remedies of time, space and talking to the trees.

When I emerged, blinking, into the bright light of life in England, I felt just like Rip van Winkle, waking up after a sleep of thirty years. England had changed and so had I, but we had gone in opposite directions. Compared to the laid-back lifestyle and gentle spirituality of the Algarve, and the idyllic sojourn on the Andean island, modern life now seemed noisy and negative, aggressive and materialistic. This was a steep learning curve.

I went back to Dr Keith Hearne, my UK hypnotherapy teacher and mentor, with whom I had studied over the years and who had taught me much about past life regression. With him I refreshed and updated my professional training and started working from a local Natural Healing Centre.

I had come full circle. It had taken me three decades with many adventures, bumps and scrapes along the way. Yet with the benefit of hindsight it's clear that my strings were being pulled at every stage. If I had stayed in England, I would probably have stayed on the corporate hamster wheel and not found my spiritual pathway. The move to Spain had allowed me the challenge of setting up, running and then losing my own companies. If I had not gone to the Algarve, I would not have started my spiritual journey or been exposed to so many wonderful places, people, practices and possibilities. In Berlin I tasted wealth but only as an *amuse bouche* before the rug was pulled again. I had to be back in England, returning to my spiritual pathway and continuing my development.

My true work is healing and being of service and it is here that I need to be. Past life regression work is my passion. As well as Ron Pittendrigh and Dr Keith Hearne, from whom and with whom I learned so much, I have studied and worked with various masters including Roger Woolger and Judy Hall, and I have worked in many interesting places such as the College of Psychic Studies in London.

My best teachers, though, have been the thousands of clients I have worked with over the years. These have been 'ordinary people' who, in their quest to resolve an issue that was holding them back, worked with me and found the root causes of their problems back there in past lives.

When I work with a new client, I always explain exactly what they can expect – and not everyone is comfortable with what I do. There are many hypnotherapists around and, from what I've heard, nobody else works quite as I do, way out there in the long grass as it were. I like to explain the broad concepts of reincarnation, of life before life and also of life between lives, because when a client takes a past life journey it is what I call 'the cycle of the soul'.

What does this mean? The client starts off in this life, I put them into a deep state of relaxation and from there through a doorway of their choosing into a past life. I will make contact with the past life character and establish who they are before moving them forward to find the next important event in that life. That is why, in my stories, you will read references to a doorway, to moving on, and phrases such as "I next met Darius five years later", which indicates that the character has moved forward.

The end of that life is of course always important, especially how the character died: is it at home surrounded by family and friends or is it in the thick of battle or being dumped over the side of a pirate ship? Whatever the circumstances, that is the time closest to the soul leaving the body so it leaves a fresh imprint. I always invite the character to review their life too and this is their chance to voice regrets or misgivings, joy or sadness, resentment or hatred. And I always ask for 'the passing thought', the thought that's carried forward at the point of that final breath. This could be, for instance, "Thank goodness it's over" or "I'm at peace now". Sometimes it could be, "I'll get even with him if it's the last thing I do!"

For example, one man I worked with had a good job and a happy, settled family life. He was in his late forties and explained that he was aware of himself being too aggressive and overbearing at work, even though this was not his usual self.

"I always feel I have to prove myself," he said, "even though I know I am doing a good job."

We found a past life where he had been a Roman soldier, training to join the elite force of the army. The training was long and hard and one of the challenges was to climb a cliff face with a heavy load on his back. He was tired and he was struggling. As he got one hand over the top of the cliff to pull himself up onto the land, his commander was there shouting, "You're not good enough, you're too weak!" With that, the commander stamped on the man's hand and kicked his head, causing him to fall back off the rock face and into the sea below. The soldier's passing thought was, "I will never be weak again."

Once a character has died in a past lifetime, I encourage the soul to leave the body and converse with me, reviewing that lifetime from its new perspective. Were the goals met, were lessons learned? There can be some very insightful answers here, ranging from wasted opportunities to having done one's best. I then do healing work around the traumas of that lifetime and others.

Next, I invite the soul to 'go home' to that non-physical realm, to the life between lives, the so-called Bardo state, and to find itself at the stage of getting ready for this current incarnation. The soul will generally be preparing its plans for this lifetime with guidance from others, perhaps a 'council of elders', wise old souls whose task is to support those who are returning for another incarnation on Earth. (Interestingly, in all the years I have been doing this work only once has a client identified the elders as including any females in their number, although usually they are pure 'beings of light' rather than old men in long robes.)

In that non-physical realm, the soul is fully aware of the goals — and the challenges — it is setting for itself and has the chance to check whether anyone from its 'soul group' will be alongside. A soul group, I have learned, is a group of individuals who travel across lifetimes together. Think of the Middle Ages, when groups of actors and musicians would travel from town to town. They would arrive in town, head for the local tavern to pick up the local gossip, and then devise an entertainment for the local people based around the headlines of the day. Different members of the group would take leading roles, sometimes a musician, sometimes a poet, sometimes an actor whilst the others take supporting roles. When their time in that town was over, they would move on to the next and start all over again.

So it is with a soul group. Before the incarnation of a soul, members of the group decide who will take supporting roles and what their scripts will be. Perhaps one has to experience poverty and another has to learn about dealing with money, or one has to learn how to give love whilst another has to learn acceptance of love. They work together in a lifetime to help one another learn these lessons. So members of your soul group may be here with you in this lifetime but they are not necessarily the most loving ones; indeed, they could well be the very people who press your buttons and give you the toughest times.

When these reviews are over, I invite the soul to return to the physical body of the client on the couch, back to this current lifetime, and the cycle of the soul is complete.

Naturally, when a soul returns to this physical world for a new lifetime, it forgets all about its script! It's rather like going into a huge, strange supermarket. If you have a shopping list, you may well go direct to the items that you need, put them in your trolley, cross them off your list and go straight to the checkout. But if you've forgotten your list, you may find yourself going up and down each aisle, looking for what you need. Along the way you will see all sorts of interesting things and may decide to try something new (put them in your trolley). Some of these could turn out to be nice and you will definitely want them again, but others you would definitely not want to repeat. It may be uncomfortable and a totally different experience, not nearly as cut and dried as knowing the shopping list, yet the experience exposes us to many more choices and decisions and, in the process, we learn more about ourselves.

There are of course those who say that this whole thing is a load of nonsense, that there is no such thing as a soul let alone a panel of old men in beards helping us to prepare our script ahead of reincarnation! They may be right, but I find it interesting that therapists far more prominent in this field than me also work to similar processes and also refer to elders and soul groups. We cannot know the truth one way or the other until we are there ourselves. It is my experiences that have led me to believe that these things are so, and it is part of the framework within which I work. If clients are open-minded enough to work with me once I have explained all of that, then I ask them merely to suspend doubts for the duration of the session and see for themselves how it plays out. After all, it's the results that really matter.

A curious question arises, even for me, about the nature of time. We experience time in a linear way yet this is a worldly, human construct. Perhaps, instead, we are living all of these lives not in the past but in parallel, all at the same time. I am open to the concept of parallel lives and indeed, in these times of massive energy shifts, I know people who have time-shifted if only for a few seconds, slipping momentarily into a parallel life. But from the point of view of therapy, and for the sake of achieving the healing that is needed, which is always my priority, it is much easier for the client and me to follow the linear model.

For instance, I once worked with a lady in the Algarve who was curious to know more about her past lives and to experience one. During the course of an afternoon, three lives were discovered in reverse chronological order, her most recent first and then working backwards. The first life was that of a young maiden, the daughter of a merchant, who was at a May Fair. She had a garland in her hair as the May Queen and the festivities included dancing around the maypole, with music and eating and drinking.

Then we met a very rough character, a man who told me he worked with pigs and that he was dying of swine fever. My client started coughing at this point. Trying to ascertain a timeframe, I asked if there was a king or queen on the throne.

"A king," came the reply. I asked his name and whether the was a good king. "Henry. He's a pig. I live with pigs, our king is a pig and pigs are going to be the death of me!" he wheezed.

As soon as we moved to another life the client's breathing eased and the coughing stopped. This third life was long ago, around 830 CE. I met a young woman in Ireland who was waiting for her betrothed to arrive home. He had been fighting in England, his boat had landed safely and he was riding to be with her at her castle where a feast awaited. The young woman gave me a detailed description of her family crest and that of her husband-to-be, and explained how the servants had prepared a pig and were cooking it in a pit cut into the ground and covered over. She gave me the name of the village (it was an odd name I had never heard before) and told me that there wasn't really a beach even though they were close to the coast. Rather, there were dunes and marshes that led into the sea.

There were several interesting points to come out of that session. Firstly, the client's husband (who had declared that this was all a load of rubbish) had been sitting at the other end of the room throughout with the full knowledge and permission of the woman and me. He was under strict orders not to say a word, whatever he saw or heard, and had been taking copious notes all the way through. Afterwards, he admitted that he was amazed especially when his lovely wife, who had a beautifully modulated English voice, started swearing as the pigman and wheezing as well. He emailed me a few days later to say that he had actually found the village in Ireland that the young woman had mentioned and it was exactly as had been described.

Secondly, what a wonderful variety of lives: a merchant's daughter in the wealthy shires of England, a rough pigman and a lord's daughter in southern Ireland. Had the client really been all those people? Or was she really living all of those lives right there and then as she lay on the couch, as well as her current one? I have no idea, but it certainly makes my life easier to deal with them one at a time.

CHAPTER 3

Food Issues and Weight Loss

Perhaps not surprisingly in modern times, I have had many, many clients coming to me for help with losing weight. They are mainly women and I sympathise, being a large lady myself. My own mother was Austrian, a true Brunhilda type, and I have her build. I've had my own issues with food and have indeed discovered a few past lives in which I starved to death – not a pleasant way to go.

These clients tell me that they have tried every diet going, they have been to the gym every day, and still nothing works. I understand because I have done all that too. My clients' experience and mine tells me that, almost invariably, the real underlying root causes of someone holding on to too much weight has nothing to do with how often we go to the gym or how many calories we eat. The issue is at an emotional level. Let me first make it clear that, when dealing with a client who has weight issues, I always check the medical history, ask whether there are any other underlying conditions, whether the client has considered nutrition, allergies and so on.

In fact, my approach to weight loss is not just to look at past lives, although that is very often where the journey takes us. I sometimes even talk to the body too – there is an example of that in Monica's story, later. Sometimes I talk to the brain in our gut, called the enteric nervous system. I usually call it Eric for short and Eric has a direct line via the vagal nerves to the brain in our head. These nerves are part of the parasympathetic nervous system and it has been scientifically shown that far more messages go from Eric to the head brain than in the other direction. It has also been shown that we 'hear' or 'feel' through our gut a split second before our other head brain senses. We're all familiar with this. We may have a gut reaction about a person or a situation, we feel gutted if something goes wrong and we have butterflies in our stomachs when we are nervous or excited. That's Eric at work.

It is Eric who controls the activity around the stomach area including the digestive system and the colon. It is Eric who senses whether something we have eaten is not good for us and needs to be expelled, deciding whether to send it back up or down and out. So Eric can play an important role in any issues to do with food and digestion and it would be disrespectful to leave him out of negotiations.

I will also talk directly to the excess weight, to find out why it is hanging around; very often it has been built up as a buffer zone or as protection. Let me give you an example. An attractive woman is in a happy relationship with a man. Something happens, they split up and she is emotionally distraught. At some level, the psychological reasoning could go like this:

'My man wanted me because I was attractive. Then he left me and that was very painful. I don't want to go through that again so if I make myself less attractive no man will want me and then I won't get hurt anymore.'

The common Western stereotype of 'an attractive woman' has been one who is slim so, by putting on weight, some women feel they will be less attractive and therefore less desirable. Sometimes a woman will put on weight, either consciously by eating the wrong foods or simply overeating or unconsciously because her body has picked up the message to put on weight.

Adding a layer of weight can sometimes be protection from physical, mental or emotional abuse too. This is actually protecting the key chakras, or energy centres, against attack; there is much information about chakras to be found on the Internet and some of them are key to weight issues. The sacral chakra is located in the abdomen, the lower back and sexual organs, and it is related to emotions and sexuality. It has an association with the element of water. The solar plexus, just above the navel, has fire as its element and it relates to personal power and will but also to the metabolism.

Those who have suffered emotional trauma or sexual abuse could well want to protect the sacral chakra. Those who have been the victim of mental or verbal abuse, or fallen prey to a narcissist, or been kept imprisoned physically or psychologically, would want to protect the solar plexus. Talking to the excess weight, finding out what purpose it is serving and, when the healing has been done, giving it permission to go with 'mission accomplished' is a powerful process. It also allows those chakras to reactivate and put the body back into balance.

The relevance of past lives is this: if the passing thought of someone who is starving to death is, 'I will never go hungry again', then that is the message the soul carries into the next lifetime and the next until that trauma is healed. Over the years I have worked with so many women who will open their handbags and show me that they are carrying food with them. At one level, they cannot rationalise it. Let's face it, most of us don't have to go far nowadays before we find somewhere to buy food of one kind or another. But at a deeper level these women can't help themselves. It's a comfort blanket, a reassurance. To me, this is a clear echo from a past life and not having enough to eat.

Historically, there were of course many reasons why people would starve to death. Going back to ancient times, life was one long battle for survival. If people could not kill an animal or find enough fruit or vegetables to eat and store for the winter months, they would starve. Throughout history there have been famines. People were thrown into prisons and left to die. These circumstances were not unusual. Painful, yes, and very traumatic but not unusual.

Stacey was in her early thirties when she came to see me, a lovely lady who was clearly overweight. She told me she had cravings for all the wrong foods, knew she was eating wrongly but could not do anything about it. There were factors in this lifetime that would have contributed to some of those issues but nevertheless she happily agreed to explore a past life.

We met a young lady who introduced herself as Sarah Clark (or perhaps Sara Clarke). She said she was twenty-two years-old and that the year was 1765. Sarah was at the local market but she couldn't give me the name of the town. She wanted bread but didn't have any money.

"We don't have money," she explained. "We are a poor family. Everyone's poor." She said that King Henry was on the throne – she could not specify which Henry he was – but that he was not a good king. "The rich people have money and nobody else does."

Sarah's husband John was a carpenter who made tables and chairs. He was a good carpenter and he was at the market trying to sell his furniture, but nobody could afford to buy it. They had no children. Sarah and John lived in a very small house and Sarah did not have work; she just spent her days trying to find food as there was never enough money.

When I next met Sarah a couple of years later, John was sick and then he died, the cause of death not specified. Sarah was back in the market but something had changed. Since John had died nobody wanted to know her and everyone was staying away from her.

"They don't like me anymore. They're shouting at me, they're mad, they don't want me there," complained Sarah. "But they know me. I don't understand."

She missed her husband very much. She had to go to the market every day to try to find or beg food just to survive, and this was made much more difficult with the hostility she now faced. She told me she was very weak and very tired and didn't have the energy to go on like that anymore. At the time of her death, Sarah was just twenty-five years-old.

"I'm at home, in a dirty bed, everything is so dirty... I'm cold, so cold... I can't move, I want to get up but I can't move."

Before she passed, I asked Sarah to review her life. She was confused.

"Why did this happen? I've never done anything, I've never hurt anyone... Why is this happening?"

Sarah also had a message for Stacey, her future self.

"You're not like me. You have so much more. You're not poor, you have things, possessions. I never had much, I never had anything. You do."

I asked Sarah what lessons she had learned from that lifetime. Her response was very clear.

"People don't like things they don't understand. I was just sick, I was not bad. They were not really my friends, they were horrible."

When we followed Sarah's soul back to the time when it was preparing for this present incarnation, I asked what had been in mind for this current life.

"I haven't made it easy for myself. It will be hard. Why would I decide to do that? Why not make it easy?" And the advice to herself was, "It won't be easy but it will not always be hard. You have to learn strength. You will become stronger. There will be hurdles and you have to get over them. Go and live it."

A lot of healing work was done with Sarah, and therefore with Stacey too, at that soul level and it had a positive effect. She later messaged me to say that finding out about the life as Sarah had really resonated with her – and that something had shifted. Her eating habits had changed and she felt much more in control of her food intake. The desperation had gone.

Sometimes, even when the intention is for the client to go back to a past life, their unconscious has other ideas. When this happens, I always follow. After all, the client's unconscious, or higher self, knows what is needed far more clearly than I do!

Tracey came to see me with issues of anxiety as well as wanting to lose weight. She was in her early fifties, mother to three active youngsters, and had reached a stage where life in general was all getting a bit too much for her. Earlier work with her had led to her being more relaxed and her sleep had improved. Now it was time to tackle the weight.

Tracey went into the deep state of relaxation easily, being used to the process by now, and I encouraged her to find a door that would lead her into a past life. It soon became evident to me that this was not the route that her unconscious wanted to take, so I had a quick chat with it and then talked to Eric, the brain of the gut. He told me, and thus Tracey, that there was a lot of self-sabotage going on around certain issues in her life.

"I can see a circle going round and round, and there's a big knot in it," Tracey said in that deep state of relaxation. Eric explained that the knot represented Tracey holding on to things, preventing things from flowing as they should.

I told Tracey to go back to the first time there was a knot in her stomach and she found two events straight away. In one, she was a little girl at primary school. It was lunchtime and the little boy sitting opposite her was sick all over the table; after that, she couldn't go to the canteen for her lunch for a week. In the second event, also when she was a little girl, she was riding her bike on a path while her mother was walking with her. Somehow, her mother went ahead and Tracey lost sight of her.

"I thought I was lost," said Tracey. "Mummy was out of sight, I thought she was gone."

I went through a process to allow Tracey to release these and all other thoughts around food and abandonment, and then went back to Eric. He was clearly in charge of the session so I asked what other issues were holding Tracey back. 'Gratification' was next on the list. In her deeply relaxed state, Tracey's unconscious knew the answer.

"If I don't make myself feel better with food, nobody else will. I need to cheer myself up as nobody else will."

Clearly, both physical and emotional levels were involved in this.

I asked Tracey to go back to the first time she felt she had to fend for herself because nobody else would look after her, and this time she went straight back to a past life. We met a soldier called Jacques right at the end of his life. He was on a battlefield, had no idea where, and he had been wounded in the chest. From his voice, it was clear that Jacques was weak and he was coughing. He had been left to die where he lay as the troops moved on. Taking Jacques to the point of his death, I asked him to review his life.

"It was a life well lived. I was strong, I was a servant. I don't deserve this, I've been abandoned." His passing thought was, "This battle was for freedom. Now this is setting me free."

We did some healing work around those key phrases of not being deserving and being abandoned, and then returned to Eric who suggested that 'Reproduction' was another important factor.

"The work is done," explained Tracey's unconscious, "so there's no need to try. The babies have been nurtured and brought forward, they don't need my sustenance any more. That makes me sad." At this point, tears rolled down her cheeks. "There's a sensation of coming rejection. I have to go through the process of them leaving. I know it's right, it has to happen…" Her voice tapered off into a big sigh.

When was the first time she had felt the loss of a child? Again we found a past life.

"I can see a young woman sitting and cradling a new-born baby that's died." That young woman introduced herself as Sarah, who was holding her first child, a little girl who did not have a name. "I don't know what to do with it, I've wrapped it in my apron."

Sarah told me she was around twenty years of age. She had no idea where the baby's father was and could not tell me if she was married. Moving Sarah forward to the point of her death, she was fifty-six and not very well. That first child was buried outside the house she lived in. She said she lived a simple life and she'd had other children and a happy home.

"I'm grateful for what I had. I'm at peace. I'm ready for whatever comes next," was her passing thought.

Healing work around all of that, Eric reported that our work at that level was done so I turned my attention to the excess weight and had a conversation with it.

"I'm comfortable here," it told me. "It's familiar, it's warm. She doesn't need me anymore but I like being here." Then Tracey's unconscious joined in the conversation! "It protects me from having to try and be a young, beautiful thing. I can hide behind it."

I confirmed to the excess weight that its job was done, and made strong suggestions to encourage it that really it was time to go now. Next, I talked to the heart.

"I'm feeling heavy right now," the heart responded. "I want to get well again. I'm not badly damaged, I'm just not on top form. I've been ignored, I need more air, more movement." At this point, Tracey was gasping for air and her body was twitching. The element associated with the heart chakra is air, and the heart is related to self-acceptance and, of course, love. We did healing work here.

FOOD ISSUES AND WEIGHT LOSS

It had been quite a session. After a process of bringing in cleansing, healing and grounding energies, I asked Tracey, who was still in that deep state of relaxation, to look at herself in a full-length mirror and see her true self. As she stepped into that new persona, full of bright new energy, there were lots of positive suggestions to support all of the work that had been done.

This was an example of letting the client's unconscious set the agenda and of following that lead. It was multi-level working that included regression both in this life and to the past. Tracey was able to go back to find relevant past lives. But we did not need to experience the whole life, only the very end in the case of Jacques, and a trauma and a happier ending in the case of Sarah. The result was a lighter, brighter and more confident Tracey, with a far deeper understanding of how she came to be in her situation and, just as importantly, how to avoid it in the future.

It shows how complex eating and weight issues can be, yet also how effective this approach can be, patiently unravelling all of the threads back to their source and healing each one in turn.

Barbara was another lady who came to see me to resolve her weight issue. She had just turned forty and had a long history of struggling to control her weight, reaching the point of wanting to sort it out once and for all.

She regressed smoothly and easily into a past life where we found Florence Welby, who was then seventeen years-old. Florence was barefoot and could not tell me what other clothes she was wearing. She was a kitchen maid, working in a house that sounded like 'Gattersby House' in Norfolk. She could not tell me which year it was. She worked with Head Cook Martha and said that the work was all right and that they treated her well.

I next found Florence in bed in a shabby room, having a baby. The story emerged that Florence had had 'a bit of fun' in the stables

41

that resulted in her becoming pregnant. She was dismissed from the big house and was now in that small room at the top of another house; she was unable to tell me whose house it was. The father of the child was nowhere to be seen. Florence died in childbirth there, all alone, feeling totally abandoned at just twenty-four years-old.

"At least I don't have to worry anymore," was her passing thought.

Having completed the cycle of the soul with Barbara, I turned my attention to the excess weight and asked what it was doing. It seemed very arrogant and sure of itself.

"I'm making her miserable," it said, "because I'm in charge. She can't resist things and she's been like this for twenty years now. She needs to get control of her eating. She likes eating bad things and, when that happens, it stays on. She comfort-eats, it gives her a buzz, she looks forward to eating bad things."

Barbara knew all of this, of course, that was precisely the point. What was interesting was the excess weight's attitude, really not wanting to shift.

"When she's miserable, I feel good because I've done my job," it said. "I don't want to help her."

Part of the work needed here was to change the excess weight from Mr Nasty to Mr Nice, and this meant involving other parts of the body too. I spoke with the head brain, inviting it to create new pathways, new default settings for Barbara's eating habits. The old ways had to be blocked off and permanent diversions created to steer her towards more healthy options and lighter meals. It also had to work on the very common issue of food as a reward when things go well and a comforter when things go wrong.

The heart said that it felt quite empty to start with but, after our conversation, said it felt better and was looking forward to feeling happy again. What about Eric? As always, he was key to this situation. He said it was important to get full cooperation and that he would, of course, play his part.

"I'm sure we can do it," said Eric.

It may sound like a relatively simple session, perhaps compared to Stacey's more complex and layered one. But there was a lot of negotiation involved in persuading the excess weight to change its attitude. Barbara was still hanging on to the emotions of loss and abandonment from that past life, in exactly the area where Florence held her baby.

A couple of weeks after we had finished our last session, Barbara sent me a message.

"I thought I'd send you a quick email to let you know how I'm doing after our sessions recently. I started the Cambridge Weight Plan shortly afterwards and I've lost two stones in seven weeks! It's a very low-calorie diet but I've stuck to it religiously and not strayed once! People around me can't believe I haven't binged or had a 'treat' but I truly have not strayed and I have reaped the rewards. I've got another two and a half stone to lose but feel very positive and cannot believe how well this is going for me. It's all down to our sessions so I'd like to thank you very much."

A message like that reminds me why I got into this type of work and why I am so passionate about it.

CHAPTER 4

Social History

When a client and I embark upon a journey to a past life, we have no idea where that journey will take us. Will we find ourselves in the thirteenth century or the nineteenth, or even thousands of years ago? Quite often the details are basic, the lives poor. As I have said, the objective of a session is always to resolve the issue in this life, not to have a history lesson. But sometimes we uncover a lifetime so rich in detail that it gives a real glimpse into the social history of the time, as well as providing valuable insights into the challenges this time round.

Charlotte was just fifty when she came to see me. A wealthy and highly successful woman, she had faced and overcome a number of professional and personal obstacles in her life. She was on her spiritual pathway and had already experienced brief flashbacks to previous lives. Because of this, she wanted to know what could be gleaned from exploring more fully a past life that might help her move forward in this one.

Because of her regular meditation practice, Charlotte slipped very easily into a deep state of relaxation and then into a past life. As usual, my first question was what she was wearing on her feet.

"Pink satin bootees, and I am also wearing a pink dress with lots of ribbons and bows. And it's very itchy!"

That was my introduction to Melissa, then aged four. Melissa explained that she was being carried and swung around by a man who was making her laugh. This was her father, a young man with a moustache who smelled of pipe tobacco. She told me that her father had brown eyes and he looked at her with love in those eyes.

Melissa explained that she was in an opulent home with long velvet drapes at the windows. It was called 'something Park' and was in East Anglia, the year being 1851. This self-assured young lady knew exactly what the situation was in the household.

"I'm very spoiled. I'm not the only child but I'm the big one, the most important one. I really want all the attention."

Her father's name was Ralph ("It's pronounced Rafe") and the surname was, she thought, perhaps Somerset. Melissa explained that her father had important genealogy.

"I have a sense of being part of an important lineage. It is important to preserve the history of the family, important for me to marry the right person." Remember, at this stage, Melissa is only four years-old. Next I asked if there was a king or a queen on the throne and she replied, "King Edward," and then paused. "I'm not sure that's right, they keep talking about Teddy."

She described her father talking to a group of men who were trying to have a serious conversation with him, but he was playing with her instead. The conversation was about politics and social nuances, who was in with whom and so on, but her father was not interested. It was clearly important for these men to make Melissa's father listen to what they had to say but he wasn't taking any notice.

"He's playing with me. He knows what they want to do. He comes across as light-hearted and gentle but he's very astute and

SOCIAL HISTORY

politically adept. He has inherited a lot of political sense from his ancestors." The visitors wanted to discuss shipping and the war, something that Melissa's father was involved with. She went on to say that the visitors "Seem very grey, civil servant types, very official. My father knows that they're constrained in what they can say and do. He's not."

I next met Melissa when she was seventeen. A maid was brushing her long brown hair and helping her dress in readiness to be presented to the Queen. Melissa described her dress as dark green taffeta with a wide square neck, off the shoulder, with some dark green velvet too. I asked if anyone was accompanying her to the event and she sighed.

"Some boy called Paul is taking me. He's got red hair. I don't like him, I find him dull. I feel like a snob saying that but it's how I feel." I wanted to know more about Paul. "It's political. He's the younger brother of someone important. He thinks he's being smooth but he's just annoying."

Melissa explained that her father had died a few years before.

"It was a bit of a mystery. He'd gone on a trip to somewhere hot and he died. He was having an affair though I don't know what makes me say that." I asked about her mother and any siblings. "I don't really like mother, she's cold, a social climber. She didn't come from the same social background as my father and she never enjoyed being a mother. I have a little sister, Pamela, who is now four, and there might be another one between us, a boy. There's something wrong with him mentally, people don't talk about him, I can see that he's a spastic. He doesn't live at home. I'm not sure where he lives."

As we were into a slice of social history, I asked Melissa to tell me about being presented to the Queen.

"There was a crash. I got thrown out of the carriage and I landed on my lower back on the kerb. I've damaged my legs, I can't walk." She said that Paul was being nice to her and she felt guilty for being nasty to him. Melissa explained that her carriage had collided with a larger moving thing – she thought perhaps it might have been a fire engine – but had very little memory of the accident. After the accident, and presumably whatever treatment was deemed possible, she was taken to the family's country house which she called something like 'Manston Park'.

After that, I met Melissa as an older lady. She was wearing, by her own description, expensive clothes and a bonnet, all very grey. She told me she had a sense of a "vast, wasted life". She was in the drawing room of her home. The curtains were drawn, the light was dim and Melissa said she was depressed. She'd clearly had a lot of time to ponder about her life and the lives of those around her.

"I can walk with calliper things," she said, "and now I feel guilty because I was unkind about my little brother. I was not nice to him when I was growing up. When I was young, I was pretty and I was well-off and I wrapped people around my finger. I was very manipulative and I feel guilty about that too now." Melissa went on to explain that she was married to a politician called John. "It might be Sir John Tyndmarsh. He is very well dressed, has good manners and can't always say what he thinks like my father. He is a genuinely lovely man and I don't deserve him. He is despairing of me, exasperated."

They had been married for thirty-five years and did not have any children. They lived in an old family home and Melissa took great pleasure from the sensuality of the house with its beautiful fabrics, furniture and floors. She told me about the embroidered cushion work on the sofa and the shape of its wooden legs. There was a quartet playing music in the house. Yet despite all the trappings that would make for a comfortable life, Melissa was depressed, and I asked what was making her feel that way.

"I feel I've let my husband down by not having children. He doesn't feel that, he enjoys my company… why do I feel so down?

I feel very guilty. I have a wonderful life and yet I can't get past the grief." I asked what it was that Melissa was grieving for.

"Something I can't even see… all I can see is a little baby's face, a baby dead in the fish pond. I feel very strangely detached, it's not real and yet it is probably my child, thirty years ago… I've felt guilty for thirty years because if I had not been so self-centred, the child would still be alive… the little boy put his arms up, he wanted me to pick him up… I didn't pay attention… it breaks my heart. I was so empty-headed. I just said, 'Not now Matthew, just stop it.' He had long, blond tousled hair…

"After the accident in the carriage, my legs were not good. Everyone said it was a miracle I had a baby. I didn't bond with him because I was young and he was inconvenient… this messy baby thing, he was disruptive… the noise, the neediness, I found it all so difficult. I didn't hate the child, I just didn't love him enough. I was quite glad he'd wandered off and I didn't have to concentrate on him.

"I didn't feel really sad when he died, just really guilty. I didn't ever tell anyone, but it was a relief when he died. It was a horrible secret to keep, horrible as a mother and also because of the family thing. Keeping the genealogy, the family history, that was important. But it wasn't, not really. There was the weight of history, the waiting and the weighting. I feel angry, I feel constricted by the whole set-up. I'm not very social but I have to do social events, I would rather be painting or reading. Young people seem to be less constrained than me."

Melissa gave the year as 1904. As she was dying, she was in her four-poster bed in her London home, 53 Wimpole Street. She was suffering from breathing problems and had a hand-pumped oxygen tank by her side. She said she felt very claustrophobic. At the point of death, I asked her to review her life.

"I wasn't very honest, really. I had privilege and opulence, and I was always brought up to be grateful for it but I always felt a void.

The religious element was disappointing. I wasn't nearly as nice a person as my father or my husband. I was much more manipulative and calculating, and I was a harsh judge of myself.

"My dear husband is here with me, stroking my hand. He's younger than me, he's very loving. He could have met someone else and had lots of children and been happy. I feel sad about that. I think he was happy with me though… he's such a nice person." Melissa's passing thought was, "I really must do better next time. I must have been such a disappointment."

The soul's review of that lifetime was interesting.

"I feel sad for her because she was lovely just as she was. She was very good at making people laugh." At this point, tears fell from Charlotte's eyes. "Some people are lovable and they don't know it. They don't have to change, it doesn't matter if they're self-centred. Just be yourself. It's okay to be very rich, it's completely okay to be very rich. It's perfectly fine to have lots of money, you don't have to feel guilty about it. Cream always rises to the top. You just have to take your place. Being a mother is not the only reason that you are worthwhile. Being well off doesn't mean you don't deserve happiness."

Melissa had set herself the goal for this lifetime to heal herself, with an emphasis on the financial aspects. The obstacles she set herself were a lack of self-belief and a deep feeling of unworthiness. The advice from the soul was, "Accept love from others. Accept wealth. It's okay to be important. Aren't you inspired by other people who have achieved things?"

All of that resonated hugely with Charlotte and the situation she found herself in at this time of her life. Clearly emotional, she told me she could identify very closely with the key elements of Melissa's life, and the goals and challenges she had set herself for this lifetime were certainly playing out. It brought a fresh level of insight and understanding to Charlotte, especially around the money issues and the notion that "it's perfectly alright to be wealthy, cream rises to the top."

Does Melissa's story check out from an historical point of view?

We met her at four years-old when she said the year was 1851 and there was a king on the throne, Edward. But then she'd paused and said, "They're always talking about Teddy." Well, Queen Victoria was on the throne from 1837 until her death in 1901, but there was a very prominent politician around at the time, who came from one of the oldest, wealthiest and most powerful families in Britain. This was Edward George Geoffrey Smith Stanley, 14th Earl of Derby, KG GCMG PC PC (Ire), no less, who was born in 1799 and died in 1869. He was Prime Minister three times, albeit for short stretches, and he was in the thick of the machinations of the Conservatives, Peelites and Liberals at the time.

From 1834 to 1851 he was known as Lord Stanley and in 1851, upon the death of his father, he assumed the title of the 14th Earl of Derby. He was a highly intelligent and principled man who introduced a state education system in Ireland and was responsible for major reforms in Parliament. His first stint as Prime Minister was in 1852, and his Chancellor of the Exchequer was Benjamin Disraeli. It is highly likely that this was the 'Teddy' being referred to.

Interestingly, when Melissa was seventeen she told me she was a debutante about to be presented to the Queen. That would be correct and she would have been presented to Queen Victoria were it not for the tragic accident in her carriage.

I could not find any details of a 'Ralph Somerset' that would match the profile given by Melissa for her father, or of 'Sir John Tyndmarsh' as her husband. That was a little frustrating. But the key point was the healing that the session brought to Charlotte and, from that perspective, it was very successful.

Toby came to see me because his life was in a mess. He was in his late twenties and had a loving family but somehow he just could not find his way forward. He said he was always looking for something more, he was never satisfied and he distanced himself from his family. He wasn't quite sure what I could do but felt that the answer was 'inside somewhere'. By the time we came to the past life session, we had already done some work and so Toby was comfortable with the process of going into a state of deep relaxation. What followed was a surprise to both of us.

A young lady introduced herself as Elizabeth. She told me she was wearing a blue laced bonnet and a laced dress but that they were "tatty", not at all presentable. She was wearing a pinafore over the dress and black, buckled shoes. I asked Elizabeth where she was and she replied that she was indoors, in a house. Was it hers?

"I wish! It belongs to the Earl. Fitzherbert, they call him Fitzy."

The Earl had a wife but no children. His wife had suffered several miscarriages and so there was no heir to the title or the estate. Elizabeth told me that the house was called what sounded like 'Tygwyn Manor', near the town of Tygwyn although the house itself was in the country. She set the year as 1911 and said that King George was on the throne.

Elizabeth was nineteen and had already worked as a chambermaid in the household for a few years. By her own admission it was a good job; she was well looked after ("That's rare in these days") and she was happy there.

She explained that the Earl was an investor, he owned several companies and was involved with politics. He was well connected and there were often dinner parties or guests for the weekend at the country house. I asked what was happening in the wider world, outside of the house.

"There is peace out there," she said, "but people talk of tensions. I don't understand, I'm not well informed, I can't pry… I'm simple, I would just love to be married and have children. I've got my eye on one of the Earl's acquaintances but it can never be. His name is von Herbert. He's kind, gentle, polite, interested and he sees people as more than just staff… that's probably just me being silly."

Two years later, times had changed.

"von Herbert's been recalled, all the Germans have gone, we're on the brink of war. He was Ambassador at the German Embassy. He's German but he speaks like an Englishmen and he's distantly related to the Kaiser and to Queen Victoria. I became his mistress. I was naïve, I was in love. I thought we could live happily ever after. A man like that doesn't fall in love with a girl like me."

Elizabeth told me that she had become pregnant and had confronted von Herbert. He didn't want to know and had in fact told the Earl something, she wasn't sure what. But the Earl made it clear that she could not stay at the house so she had to leave. She made her way to London where she found lodgings with some other women. I asked if she was working.

"Working? Well, if you call it that… myself and the other ladies work the streets at night… I've been doing this for a couple of months now. I'm still carrying the child, it's due in five months… Why am I doing this work? Because a woman's got to make a living… how am I supposed to bring up a child if I have nothing? Yes, it's a tough life but I'm not doing it for me, I'm doing it for the baby."

The irony of her being pregnant with an unwanted child, and being thrown out of the Earl's house because of it, while the lady of the house could not have children and therefore there was no heir to the Earl's title, was not lost on her. I asked Elizabeth to say more about the work she was doing. Remember that the client on the couch is a young man in his late twenties.

"I deal with anyone I can get. I prefer the professionals but they are few and far between. They treat you like a lady. I mostly deal with drunk, old smelly men falling out of taverns. I give a… well, whatever they want, for sixpence, and I charge the gentlemen a shilling. It's not so much about the money, it's how they treat you, how they make you feel, with lavish food and gifts, it's not real. I live in Soho at 143 Bishops Lane. No, the men don't go to the house, it's mostly performed out in the streets, but the gentlemen have hotels or cars or horses and carriages."

Elizabeth was still working a few months later despite being some six or seven months pregnant.

"I'm being pinned up against a wet, cold stone wall… it's night-time, it's dark… There are three men taking it in turns, they're being abusive… one's got his hand around my throat and I can't breathe. I'm worried, I'm still pregnant, I'm bleeding but they don't stop just because I'm bleeding. I'm begging them to stop but they won't, they've got me pinned.

"One's kicked me in the stomach, they're pulling my hair, they're spitting on me. They've got my feet, they're dragging me… I'm trying to get a grip on the floor but I can't, it's too wet, I can't fight back, I'm too weak… I crawl away but it's no use."

All through this, Toby was writhing on the couch.

"They've finished now. There's so much blood, there's nobody to help, if there was they ignored my screams for help, the crying, the beating. I'm so alone, I feel stupid, I should never have got to this position. I shouldn't have lied to my family, I should have told them. I was a naïve young girl in love. I thought I could do it on my own, I thought I could make it… and now the baby's not made it. It was all for nothing, stupid girl."

Two days later, Elizabeth was in bed at her lodgings.

"I can't really walk, the bleeding won't stop. I've not seen a doctor, I can't afford one and I'm too ashamed to go to the hospital. My friends are not looking after me… they're not friends, just acquaintances, it's a dog-eat-dog world here. I feel hollow, ashamed, embarrassed. I've lost everything."

At the point of her death, I asked Elizabeth to review her life.

"I wish I'd done it differently. Family, they mean everything, I shouldn't have pushed them away. I threw my whole life away for one mistake, all for the sake of saving face." Her passing thought was, "I should have been more sensible. I should have found a good partner and settled down and had a contented life. I'm regretting my poor choices. I should have embraced my family."

The soul's review of that lifetime echoed Elizabeth's final realisations.

"Family is everything. They are always there for you even when you believe they're not, that was the lesson. Pick your partners carefully. Know that you have a good thing when you have it. Don't throw it away."

The goals for this lifetime were to embrace your family, let people in and don't put pressure on yourself. Be content. The challenges would be to do with money and work, pride and wanting to do it all alone, not letting people in, having unconditional love for your family and accepting them for who they are.

Toby was surprised, to say the least, that he had lived a life as a woman and, not only that, as a prostitute. He had indeed been playing out some of these patterns of behaviour with negative consequences. He had not made good choices in his relationships; he was unable to settle in any one job, however much he liked it and however much potential he could see in it; and he was aware that he was alienating his family by his actions.

He saw clearly that Elizabeth's naïvety and decision to become the mistress to a high-ranking German acquaintance of her boss had had far-reaching, devastating consequences. Elizabeth was not a bad person yet she ended up on the streets of London, prostituting herself when she was heavily pregnant because her pride prevented her from reaching out to her family. She met a violent, tragic end, having been gang-raped and beaten up. Interestingly, in this lifetime, Toby admitted that he was ambivalent about sex and did not feel at all engaged or committed when he had sex with his girlfriend. Could that be an echo of Elizabeth's feelings as a prostitute?

The advice to self had been to embrace your family, let people in, don't put pressure on yourself to succeed, and to be content. In our first session Toby had admitted he felt guilty about not being close to family and friends. He also felt guilty because he recognised that he was selfish: he did not look at the consequences of his actions, he didn't care, and he didn't do things for other people unless there was a personal gain.

Elizabeth lived her short life at a pivotal time in twentieth century history, the build-up to the start of World War I in 1914. One always has to remember that the world is seen through the eyes of that character. A simple chambermaid such as her would have a very different view to, shall we say, those of her employer the Earl Fitzherbert or her lover Ambassador von Herbert. The knowledge, understanding and perspective of events going on around them would be coloured by the lens through which they were viewed.

The other historical details? She said that the large house she worked in was called Tygwyn, or that's what it sounded like when she said it. It is a very Welsh name and there is indeed a property called Ty Gwyn Manor, in Lisvane, Cardiff. But this is probably not where she worked. She said she worked for the Earl Fitzherbert, or 'Fitzy' to his friends. There is a prominent old English family called Fitzherbert and one branch were the Fitzherberts of Tissington Hall, in Derbyshire. They would certainly have moved in those influential business and political circles. Is it possible that simple Elizabeth was trying to say 'Tissington' and I misunderstood what she said?

In any event, my emphasis is not completely on historical accuracy but rather on finding the root cause of the issues holding back the client in this lifetime and healing them at source. With that as the objective, it really does not matter if Elizabeth got the name of the house wrong. What matters is allowing her to tell her story, uncovering the traumas and going through the process of healing. After all, she was right about there being a George on the throne in 1911 as George V was crowned in June of that year.

The German Ambassador to England from 1901 to 1912 was Paul Wolff Metternich and he was replaced, for just one year, in 1912 by Adolf Marschall von Bieberstein. Does that mean Elizabeth was wrong? Maybe. Or perhaps her lover was not the actual ambassador but another high-ranking official in the embassy whose name is not recorded. Might the lover even have used a false name?

On the other hand, it is certainly a coincidence that the Earl is Fitzherbert and the lover is von Herbert.

And what was the outcome of this powerful session for the client?

"It is easier for me to accept who I am now," he said when he returned for a new session. "I am happy with who I am. And my family and friends tell me I am easier to get on with." He moved back in with his parents and mended many fences before he went travelling to take time out, broaden his horizons and, cliché though it is, to find himself.

CHAPTER 5

Defending My People

The trauma of war is immense. Those of you whose parents or grandparents were involved in the World Wars will know that they rarely talked of what they saw, what they went through. It was too horrifying. There was no counselling, just a large whisky and back to the trenches.

War itself has changed of course, with long-range missiles and weaponised drones lessening the need for hand-to-hand conflict. With television news footage, films and social media coverage, we have perhaps become immune to, detached from, the horrors of war.

But that does not mean that the soul is immune or detached. Trauma inflicted in one lifetime will be carried forward until it is healed. It may lie dormant for lifetimes until something triggers it, but it is there, rumbling gently like a volcano ready to erupt at any time.

There is also another aspect to such trauma, which is fascinating but outside the remit of this book, being the trauma passed down through generations. There's an increasing number of studies showing that trauma can be inherited in our DNA. For example, the studies carried out in the United States by the Icahn School of Medicine at Mount Sinai and the James J Peters Veterans Affairs Medical Center in New York, et al, have established that those who survived the Holocaust have altered level of circulating stress hormones compared with other Jewish people of the same age who were not involved then. Bruce Lipton's work on epigenetics explains all of this and more.

Diana was in her mid-forties when she came to see me. She had heard about past life regression work and had been recommended to me by a friend of hers who had also been a client of mine. Diana explained that there were 'no particular issues' to be resolved but that her life seemed very complicated, with relationships at the centre of it all. She was curious to see what insights, if any, a past life would reveal. She was new to this work but, as we both discovered, a natural at allowing herself to sink into a deep state of relaxation and she easily found the door she wanted to go through. We met a man from very ancient times who gave his name as Alba.

"I have big hairy feet, very long manky toenails, claw-like, like a beast's feet. They are knobbly and very ugly. I am very hairy and I am very dirty."

Alba explained that he was in what sounded like a tropical jungle, with lush undergrowth and vines growing down.

"I'm chewing on grass, there's dirt on the ground. I'm watching and waiting for something. I'm trying to keep still. There are people behind me, hiding. I'm feeling protective, I'm braced ready for action... I have to use my instincts. I use them a lot, not my intellect. There's a group of other people here, I'm responsible for them, it's my tribe. I have very strong arms, I rip things apart, that's why I'm here.

"There's a very loud noise. Everyone is scared, including me, but I can't be scared or else I can't do what I'm meant to do. It's possibly a very large bird that kills people. They want to run in panic, but that would make it worse. I feel the panic…"

When it was over, I met Alba again.

"We're on a cliff looking down. We're free. I'm seeing something in the distance, the bird has taken somebody away. It's sad but it means everyone else is safe. The someone taken is someone I love—" Diana had tears streaming down her cheeks at this point "—but I'm not allowed to show it. I'm very sad about it but we know it means the bird will be gone for a while, there will be peace for a while…"

I asked Alba about the person who was taken.

"I feel very connected to this person, part of me has gone with them. It's my sister or my wife. She's gone and I'm watching her go. I know she's scared and I'm imagining her being eaten, destroyed. I can't do anything. I'm in shock, paralysed, and I hate myself because I can't do anything. I should have fought it and I didn't. I'm not enough. I should have been enough. I hate myself for that. I feel so angry, I want to rip it apart, get my hands on it and rip it apart. It's gone and I feel so angry, so angry…"

I asked Alba to move forward to the next important event in his life but Diana's unconscious or higher self had other ideas and we skipped instead to another life, a total contrast to that of Alba.

"I'm sitting cross-legged on a rock, meditating. I'm some sort of yogi. I'm feeling peaceful. There are white flowers around me. I have dark skin, Indian this time, grey in my hair. I'm feeling very peaceful… There is gold light in front of me. I'm experiencing enlightenment. I'm feeling very open to divine consciousness pouring into me. I'm feeling very awake, I'm leaving my body… I'm going into the universe, I'm feeling bliss, I feel whole…"

The soul told me that the goals for this current lifetime were to achieve great peace and serenity, completion, and 'to save myself'. When I asked about challenges, there was a big sigh.

"I need courage, great courage to progress. There is a great wall of fear to face and great pain. There is quite a task. I'm walking a lot, many steps… it won't be my last incarnation…"

The energy shift in Diana between her experience as Alba and her experience as the yogi was palpable. From fear, anger, worthlessness and a desire to 'rip it apart' to complete bliss, serenity and peace. What a complete turnaround and a wonderful example that shows us that not all lives are traumatic.

During the course of that session, fragments of two more lives were uncovered, fleeting glimpses that were teasingly shown and then pulled away. There was an enormous amount of healing work done around the trauma in all of the lifetimes that we were shown and those we were not shown. For someone who had never done any work like this before, Diana showed a natural aptitude which was surprising to us both.

She identified clearly with aspects of Alba: wanting to protect her tribe, her children in this life, the loss of a loved one and the feeling of helplessness that went with it as well as the strong emotions of not feeling good enough, raging against that unknown 'something'. She laughed when she said she felt much more Alba than Zen at that time in her life, but she also very much enjoyed the feeling of connecting with that universal energy and said she would try to reconnect with it.

Early thirties Hayley came to me because, as she said, "I need to sort myself out." There were all sorts of things happening in her life to do with work, relationships and money, and it was all becoming overwhelming. It was a situation I'm sure many can relate to.

By the time we came to do a past life session she was a bit more comfortable with the idea of allowing herself to go into a deep state of relaxation. Indeed, she said, she would love to relax but it was not always easy for her. With some encouragement, she reached 'the zone' and found the door to the past life her unconscious or higher self had chosen.

We met a man called Paul who told me that the place he was in was "…cold, dark, horrible, like a tomb. I can move but I can't get out. It's a kind of dungeon, it's slimy and cold and smells of mould and urine… I've been here a very long time and I just want to die." I asked Paul to tell me the story of how he came to be there. "I didn't do anything wrong," he said straight away. "There were nasty men, an army that took everything and killed a lot of people. I tried to fight. I was head of the village. An army came from far away… white people, Dutch people… I'm in Zimbabwe. The white people came and took everything, killed everyone they could find.

"They want something from me, that's why they haven't killed me yet… they want me to tell them the location of something. Maybe diamonds?" There was a pause, as though Paul was wondering whether he wanted to tell me anything more. "I know where they are but I won't tell them anything. I want to be dead. I feel angry, guilty, helpless and hopeless. I couldn't stop them…"

At the end of his life Paul was still in that dungeon, which he said was part of a complex of caves. He was cold and he was starving. I asked him to look back on his life.

"Perhaps I should have tried something else, not to fight but to talk to those people… fighting doesn't work… they forced me to fight." His passing thought was one of sadness. "I lost my wife and my children… it was too harsh."

The soul's review of that lifetime echoed Paul's thoughts in his last days. "It was a tough life, he tried but he couldn't do it. Stop fighting, go away, run away, but fighting is not right."

The healing process including gathering a lot of guilt from many lifetimes where similar scenarios had played out and the feeling of not being good enough was strongly imprinted.

Hayley had no links to Zimbabwe other than having been there on holiday and had no family links to The Netherlands or elsewhere in Africa as far as she was aware. We both noticed that Paul had called the country Zimbabwe rather than Rhodesia, which it would have been known as before independence from the United Kingdom in 1980. Historically, the Dutch had a presence in South Africa from 1652 when their first settlement was established in Cape Town. Certainly, the area now known as Zimbabwe, the former Southern Rhodesia and Zambia, is rich in diamonds and it would be highly likely that battles would have been fought with much bloodshed in order to find the source of these prized stones.

In a separate session with me, Hayley found another warrior life far away from the diamond fields of Zimbabwe. We had been discussing anxiety and, especially, an incident with her parents that had provoked a big argument. By now more used to the process of deep relaxation, I asked Hayley how she was feeling.

"I feel like I'm suffocating, there's heaviness on my chest, I want to escape... it's painful, I can't breathe..." I asked her to follow that feeling, to go back to the time when she first felt like that. "I'm in a cell underground, a tomb, I've been buried alive..." I asked this character to introduce himself and he said he was John.

"I was a warrior trying to save my people from something bad, an invading army. We are poor people with shabby clothes. We have our land and we have our horses, and we tried to save our village. These people want to destroy us... I failed to defend my people. I was the leader, a king, they all followed me. There were hundreds of huts in the countryside but there was not enough food...

"This army is from a different king. They have shining horses, they are well fed, we can't do it, we can't fight. They want to rape our women and kill our children and set everything on fire... They caught me and put me underground in this tomb. I could hear people crying, then they faded as some died. I couldn't see them but I could hear them screaming. They are going to leave me here to starve to death. It's cold, it's stone, it's hard. I want to get out but I know I can't get out, it's too small, the stone is crushing my chest."

I ask John about his flag and about the other king who attacked his village.

"My flag is a red and white cross." Here Hayley raised her arm and drew a St Andrew's cross like that on the current Scottish saltire. "The other king is Charles something. His flag is dark, black, there's something like a star or a moon on the flag. His army is all dressed in black. They come from somewhere else, they don't speak the same language as we do." He gave the year as perhaps 1592 and said he was possibly in Scotland.

At the end of his life in that miserable tomb, I asked John what his passing thought was and he replied that he had "failed". The soul's review of the lifetime was interesting. "It was short, it was difficult, it was tough. He was brave, he tried everything he could to protect his family, his tribe, but it was too much, he couldn't win. That's the lesson: you can't always win. You can always be brave, but you can't always win."

I asked the soul about one particular issue that Hayley had brought up, that of fear of commitment in her relationship. I could almost sense the soul smiling as it replied.

"His wife and his children were killed. He lost everything. Does that not explain?"

When I next saw Hayley, I asked how the experiences of that session had settled down with her. She replied that she had been tired, which is not unusual after deep and intense work, but felt as though a huge weight had lifted off her chest. That would make perfect sense, that was the stone that was crushing John in the tomb. Hayley also said that some things had fallen into place, there had been more peeling of the emotional onion, more 'Aha' lightbulb moments.

Linda was just fifty when she came to see me, having met me at the College of Psychic Studies in London. There were a number of issues on her shopping list: weight, anxiety and general problems around her stomach area where there had been some surgical interventions. She had reached the point of realising that whatever she had tried at a physical level had not worked. She had to go deeper to find an answer.

She slipped easily into a deep state of relaxation and quickly found a past life. We met a woman who told me she was wearing sandals and a robe with a brown belt. She had a gold bracelet and a gold band around her head. This woman introduced herself as Aleu (that is what it sounded like). I asked Aleu to describe for me where she was and she replied that she was outdoors in the open air, she could see land and sea. It was warm and sunny. I asked if this was her home.

"I own it, I am the queen of this land." The Lord of All Lands was her father and she said the country was Greece. Her country, perhaps one of the islands, was wealthy and strong, defended by fortresses. Aleu said that she was in her twenties and that she ruled her country alone because her husband was away. "I am strong," she told me, "and my country is at peace."

I met Aleu some years later and much had changed.

"I was betrayed," she told me. Her country was being attacked, she saw her sea and her land on fire and fighting all around her. Many people were killed and she was not able to repel the invaders. She fought bravely but she was captured. At the very end of her life, Aleu said, "I was taken, and I was killed by a knife in my womb. I was carrying my husband's child at the time but he was not there to protect me." Her final thoughts were, "My husband, my child… I am not frightened, I die with pride, I will not close my eyes, I will look at them."

The soul's review of that lifetime was insightful and, as the soul spoke, Linda had tears falling down her cheeks.

"Have no fear. You are strong. You will survive. You have strength, you have power. You can heal, you are safe."

When the soul was preparing the 'script' for this current lifetime, it listed her goals as these: to overcome, to become true, seek glory and joy, to soar and to glide, to overcome the enemies and to see them for what they are, to become the queen once more.

Although it was not the longest or most involved of past lives, it was clearly emotional for Linda.

"I have seen that queen in my dreams," she told me. "I know her."

The way that the queen was killed, with the knife through the stomach killing both her and the child in her womb, had echoed in this lifetime with stomach and womb issues.

I did not see Linda for a couple of months after that. When she returned she said that she'd felt really good after the session and things had fallen into place. She had been away on holiday for the first time in a long while, to another Mediterranean island, and felt very relaxed and rested when she returned. Several people said that she had lost a lot of weight. She told me she felt very well, very calm, and knew that she was looking much better. The queen was ruling once again.

Chrissy came to see me when she was in her mid-fifties. Her issue was relationships, with men and with food. Neither were healthy, she knew she made bad choices in both, and she was suffering physically and emotionally as a result. Although she had not done any work like this before, Chrissy found it easy to relax and she found the door to just the right past life without any problems. As usual, my first question to the character we met was what they were wearing on their feet.

"Pointed slippers. And I am wearing stockings and a tunic. I have clips in my hair. My hair is dark and shoulder length."

"Can you tell me, please, are you a man or a woman, a boy or a girl?" I asked, even though the answer seemed pretty obvious. But no.

"I am a young man," came the reply. "My name is Jarod and I am fifteen years-old."

Jarod told me he was indoors in a very large stone building, a castle, which was his home. He was not able to tell me where it was. It was springtime and out of the window Jarod could see hills in the distance. He was in his bedroom which, apart from his bed, had a couch, velvet curtains in a deep colour, a writing desk and a chair. I asked who else lived in the castle and Jarod told me there were his family and lots of servants. He said he called his father "Grandpère" whilst others addressed him as "My Lord". They called his mother "My Lady" or "Lady Jane".

Despite the plush surroundings, Jarod was not happy.

"I feel bored," he complained. "I am fed up of being here, indoors, not being free. I'd like to be outside, I need to do things. I have duties, I can't choose. There's a lot of standing around, being at my father's elbow. People such as bishops or businessmen come to the castle, they want counsel. My father is a great lord, he is a king, he has a kingdom."

I asked Jarod about life outside of the castle.

"It's peaceful out there. I don't get to see the people in the kingdom. I'm probably going to be married to a princess. I don't have any say in my life."

I next met Jarod a couple of years later when he was with his mother in the big dining hall. Jarod's father was on his deathbed and his mother was explaining to him what life would be like when his father died: the duties and expectations that would fall to Jarod to fulfil. He said that his mother was being very matter-of-fact and kind.

She told him that his father loved him very much and wanted Jarod to make him proud. Jarod went to his father's side and took his hand. His father touched his cheek and said his goodbyes, his last words to Jarod being, "Be well, be happy, be of service." I asked Jarod how he felt.

"I feel sad," he replied, "Mother feels ready, there is sadness with her, and kindness, but not grief."

There was a big burial service for Jarod's father, as befits a king, and then the coronation ceremony to crown Jarod as king.

"I have a staff to hold, I have a crown on my head now, my mother is by my side. People are presented to me, I have to put my hand on their heads… I feel detached. It all smells of lots of people, material, torches… I'm wearing a cloak and hose, shoes and breeches. I have a high-collared shirt and I am wearing my father's rings." To say that Jarod was a reluctant king would be an understatement. "People are looking at me and I'm not the man my father was. My life is not my own, I have no control. I have to be who I'm expected to be."

Moving on, I met Jarod again when he was thirty-four years-old. All was not well.

"I'm angry and I've got a headache. I'm angry at that council of people who tell me what to do. I've been passive in my own affairs, trying to be someone I'm not. These duties, they bind me, my life is empty. I'd like to be as free as the people in my kingdom, to choose where I go, who my friends are. I could trust people… I've not felt like this before. I know it's the life I was born into. I don't want just to send the army off to meet other armies, I want to be there with them."

He explained that he was in Constantinople and that his army was going to defend the city against the Trojans. "Trojans is the name for traitors, it's the traitor army. General Magdaly is leading my army. He's a good man, he's got lots of experience."

King Jarod was married to Fenula. They had two children aged five and eight, and his wife was pregnant with their third child. Their daughter was named Jane, after Jarod's mother, and the boy was named Peter. Jarod told me that he and his wife had talked about him wanting to go with the army into battle.

"She thinks I would be safer at home, but her main concern is for the children. She wishes for me to be scholarly and to be with my books. I like books, I have a fine library. I have always had men of learning visit from wider afield than the court, sometimes from other countries. My kingdom is a very pleasant place. But I'm not stupid, they present a pleasant picture. My advisers have the interests of the country at heart and sometimes they are not truly honest with me. My wife is the daughter of a trusted adviser who worked with my father. He serves at court, he has a title but very little money. Mother is still alive and, yes, I do take her counsel sometimes."

The next time I met Jarod, he was on horseback with General Magdaly, on a hillside. The armies were involved in a skirmish.

"We have chosen champions," he explained, "but two of my champions have fallen. The general says we should negotiate terms, or go to full battle if need be."

They went to battle.

"There is so much noise, so much clamour… I think of my mother, not my wife. She was so strong. I should not be here. I'm with the general, I'm fighting. People are crying all around me, there is so much noise. I feel excited and scared at the same time. I feel like I shouldn't be excited. It's my fault, I'm to blame for this. It has to be my fault. There are so many people, so much noise… I'm struck down. I leave my kingdom with my heir not old enough to rule…"

I asked Jarod to review his lifetime.

"It was a life half-lived. It was the passive life of somebody who has position and expectations put upon them. Their life is not their own. It was a bland, passive life as was expected of me. I was content with my marriage and I felt love for my parents. I regret that I did not break away in my youth and rebel, but I would not have done it to my parents and my people. Now, one reckless act will leave my kingdom and my family vulnerable." His passing thought was, "I'm sorry."

The soul's review of this lifetime was that, "It was a necessary life. It showed what was important – to live an honest life, to be true to yourself, to take pleasure from simple things. The major points were regret and passivity."

When the soul returned to the life between lives, the goals for the future were to experience fully what it is to be human, to make sure that this new lifetime is one of spiritual progression and to experience deep joy.

The messages for Chrissy were clear: don't be so passive, stand up for what you want, follow your dreams and not someone else's. The emptiness that she felt inside, and was trying to fill with physical food, could well have had echoes of that 'half-lived life' and the regret of unfulfillment. There was a very clear goal for this lifetime, to follow her spiritual pathway.

The clearing and healing work that she did on herself in the sessions she had with me did, she said, set her up perfectly for that, aligning her with what she knew deep inside.

CHAPTER 6

Reincarnation, the Concept and Early Research

What does reincarnation actually mean? It comes from a series of Latin words that translate as 'being made flesh again', or 'coming into body again'. It is the concept that humans are made up of a physical body, yes, but also a non-physical element that is variously called the spirit, soul, consciousness or essence. According to this belief, when the physical body dies the non-physical element of us survives, returns to a non-physical world or dimension and, in due course, comes back into a new-born baby for another lifetime.

There is nothing new about such belief and it is to be found at the heart of civilisations across the globe since time began. It has been embraced by all the major religions – and still is by some – and some Eastern cultures in particular take for granted the idea that the soul survives the death of the physical body.

The idea was very much alive in ancient Greek times when it was called metempsychosis and was thought of as either reincarnation or transmigration, a soul moving from animal to human life or vice versa. It was a central teaching of the Pythagorean School (c.500 BCE) of Mathematics, metaphysics and esotericism.

One legend says that Pythagoras had once been Aethalides who was a son of Hermes, messenger of the gods. Hermes allowed him one wish, anything except immortality, so he asked to be able to remember all that had happened to him, alive and dead. So it was that he remembered a life as Euphorbus, who was wounded in battle by Menelaus, King of Sparta and husband of Helen, whose abduction triggered the Trojan War. An even earlier life was much simpler, a fisherman called Pyrrhus. One can't help wondering where Pythagoras is now…

Plato, one of the most influential of classical Greek philosophers (c.428 – 347 BCE), was a student of Socrates and teacher to Aristotle. He was a strong believer in reincarnation and featured it in works such as *Phaedrus, Phaedo* and *The Republic*. Other Greek philosophers, following in the footsteps of these greats, carried forward the belief into the next centuries: Plutarch, Apollonius and Plotinus to name but a few. One of the more significant sayings of Plotinus, the founder of Neoplatonism, is:

'…*such things… as happen to the good without justice, as punishments, or poverty or disease, may be said to take place through offences committed in a former life.*'

At about the same time that Pythagoras was teaching in Greece, the Buddha was teaching in India and the concept of reincarnation was widely accepted and believed there too. The teachings of the Buddha spread far and wide in various forms and nowadays Buddhism is one of the world's largest religions. Indeed, along with Hinduism and smaller Eastern faiths such as Jainism, about half the world's population is accounted for. That's a lot of believers in reincarnation.

One of the holy books of the Hindu faith is the *Bhagavad Gita* (Song of God), and the acknowledged benchmark translation of that work was done by Sir Matthew Arnold. One relevant passage in it reads:

'Never the spirit was born; the spirit shall cease to be never; never was time it was not. End and beginning are dreams. Birthless and deathless and changeless remaineth the spirit forever. Death hath not touched it at all, dead though the house of it seems.'

The prophet Mohammed lived in the sixth century and learned about reincarnation from the Nestorian monk Bahira at a monastery in Busra. There is, however, only the odd mention of the belief in the Qur'an, or Holy Book of Islam, such as:

'God generates beings and sends them back over and over again until they return to Him.'

The concept is not taught in orthodox Islam although it does form part of Sufi philosophy.

The Druze religion, initially a breakaway from Islam, appears to bring together elements of many other faiths. Some of the basic beliefs were considered radical back in the day, some 1,200 years ago, including equality of the sexes, monogamy and the abolition of slavery. From their base in Lebanon, the Druze people moved to the mountains in the Levant where Lebanon, Syria, Jordan and what is now Israel come together, to avoid political and religious persecution and to isolate themselves.

Not only do they believe in reincarnation but also in 'walk-ins'. This is when the soul of someone who has just died is immediately reincarnated in a new-born baby. In *The Big Book of Reincarnation*, Roy Stemman quotes several of the most researched case studies from the Druze which would certainly make most people sit up and listen.[3]

Whilst reincarnation is not an official tenet of Jewish philosophy and faith, it does feature in Hasidic Judaism, which puts more

---

[3] Hierophant Publishing (2012)

emphasis on spirituality than on the strict laws of orthodox Judaism. The Hasidic belief is that souls have the ability to reincarnate in order to have experiences in various lifetimes and to learn from them. Similarly the esoteric school of Kabbalah teaches that the soul passes through a number of incarnations and has specific goals to achieve in each one.

Many people wonder why there is no mention of reincarnation in the conventional Christian Bible. The answer is that there were many references to it in the original version, but all that changed at the Second Council of Constantinople in 553 CE and only a few mentions escaped the redacting pen.

This particular thread of the rich tapestry that makes up religion today goes back to an influential Christian theologian called Origen, who lived from around 185 to 254 CE, and was a firm believer in reincarnation, as were other philosophers of this time. In his treatise *On First Principles* he wrote:

'Every soul comes into this world strengthened by the victories or weakened by the defeats of the previous life. Its place in this world as a vessel appointed to honour or dishonour is determined by its previous merits or demerits. Its work in this world determines its place in the world which is to follow this...'

Even after his death, his teachings and those of his contemporaries continued to be popular and were gaining more followers by the time of the Roman Emperor Justinian I, who ruled from 527 to 565 CE. There are differing opinions as to why Justinian took exception to Origen's teachings. Some say it was the influence of his wife, who wanted to pronounce herself a goddess, and therefore immortal, which she could not do if reincarnation were accepted. Others say he felt that if common people understood that there was indeed life after death, and another incarnation to follow, they would not be afraid of dying and would therefore be more likely to rise up and rebel. It was far better to keep his subjects in fear and ignorance!

Whatever the real reason, in a bid to stamp out the teachings of Origen, Justinian convened an ecumenical council, inviting one hundred and fifty-nine bishops from the East of the empire and only six from the West, where the teachings were better known and more popular. The emperor wanted to ensure that Origen's teachings were banned and all mention of reincarnation, or transmigration of souls, was banished from the Bible.

The Pope at the time, Vigilius, made known to Justinian that he felt there should be a fairer representation of bishops for such an important vote, and he boycotted the event despite being in Constantinople at the time. Not surprisingly, Justinian's motion was carried, and Article 1 of the 5th Ecumenical Council reads:

'If anyone assert the pre-existence of souls, and shall assert the monstrous restoration which follows from it, let him be anathema.' Note that, in those times, to be anathema meant to be cursed.

Clearly it took a long time for this to be put into practice throughout the empire, but all references to reincarnation or the pre-existence of souls were ordered to be taken out of the Bible, in what was probably one of the first major acts of censorship of its kind. And that is why the concept is far more widely known and accepted in Eastern countries than in Western nations historically dominated by Christianity.

It's strange to think that it was all that simple, isn't it? It seems hard to believe that a decision made some 1,500 years ago would have such an impact, yet it explains a lot. If there were a general acceptance by the population of the concept of life before life, it would be much easier, for example, for parents to believe a child who tells them that he or she was someone else before. In the West, most parents would brush this off as imagination or nonsense, because there is not that same precedent, widespread belief and understanding.

As we move forward in time through the centuries, we find that the concept of reincarnation did indeed survive and surfaced in the West, bringing with it other beliefs such as karma. This is the spiritual 'law of cause and effect': our thoughts and behaviour in one life determine how and when we are reborn in the next.

In some philosophies, there is even a 'ladder' of evolution whereby a soul begins in a lower lifeform, perhaps a plant, progresses to a higher one such as an animal and then becomes human. Equally, one could be demoted if behaviour was bad! The aim of eastern religions is to reach the top of the ladder, or 'get off the wheel' as some say, by reaching the state of enlightenment, Nirvana.

Madame Helena Blavatsky was born in Ukraine, then part of Russia, in 1831. A mystic, author and spiritualist, she was widely travelled and often controversial in her views that the spiritual, mystical life was more important than daily and political life. She claimed extraordinary psychic powers which were at the time investigated and branded as fraudulent. With her close companion, Henry Steel Olcott, she founded the Theosophical Society, which remains active to this day. This enigmatic figure was highly influential in her time, both in India and in Europe. She wrote several books and her teachings are still studied. About karma, she wrote:

'It is only this doctrine, we say, that can explain to us the mysterious problem of Good and Evil, and reconcile man to the terrible and apparent injustice of life… there is not an accident in our lives, nor a misshapen day, or a misfortune, that could not be traced back to our own doings in this or another life.'

Leading psychologist and psychiatrist Carl Gustav Jung defined karma as, *'a sort of psychic theory of heredity based on the hypothesis of reincarnation.'* He is also on record as saying, *'Psychic heredity does exist. That is to say, there is inheritance of psychic characteristics such as predisposition to disease, traits of character, special gifts and so on.'*

Rudolf Steiner (1861 – 1925) was an Austrian spiritualist who founded the Anthroposophy movement based on the notion that there is a spiritual world comprehensible to pure thought but accessible only to the highest faculties of mental knowledge. Transcripts of the many lectures he gave during, and especially after, the First

World War show a remarkable level of prophetic foresight into events that are unfolding now. The breadth and depth of his understanding of philosophical and esoteric matters were enormous. He often spoke about reincarnation, for example:

'The being of Gautama Buddha radiated into the Jesus child spoken of in the gospel of St Luke. The super sensible being of Buddha streamed into the astral body of the Luke Jesus child.'

'When we go through the gate of death, we leave our physical and etheric bodies, and our ego and astral body now emerge as sun and moon that have nothing to illumine.'

Steiner's book *Life Between Death and Rebirth*, a collection of talks he gave on the subject, says that the soul travels out through the planets when the physical body dies, leaving behind what he calls 'elements of our being' along the way until we reach Saturn.[4] There the soul rests until it is time for the next incarnation when it makes the return journey, picking up all the 'stuff' to bring back into the next physical lifetime.

How many people actually believe in reincarnation nowadays? The first survey on the subject was apparently undertaken by Mass Observation in 1947. It was a small survey of just five hundred respondents in a London borough and of those only four per cent said they believed in reincarnation. That number has now risen considerably, perhaps partly because people are becoming increasingly disillusioned with organised religions and are looking for 'something else'.

A survey *Views on the Afterlife* was undertaken by Pew Research Center in the USA in September, 2021, and revealed that thirty-three per cent of all American adults believed in reincarnation, although the sample size was not given on the report documents.

---

[4] New edition published by Anthroposophic Press (1968)

The fraction of believers who gave their religion as "nothing in particular" rose to forty-four per cent whilst, interestingly, the percentage rose even higher among those who classified themselves as "historically black".

In the UK, a YouGov *Death Study* conducted in March, 2021, among a sample of over two thousand residents aged sixteen and over revealed that thirty-three per cent believe in an afterlife. Of those who do believe in an afterlife, almost half think that the soul goes to "'Heaven or a similar place" where it lives on, whilst one in six believe in reincarnation. In this survey, half the respondents said, "I am not religious in any way" and, of those, almost a third believe in reincarnation.

It seems from those latest research figures that reincarnation as a concept is gaining far wider acceptance today, especially among those who do not follow an organised religion. Personally, I never ask my clients about their religion anyway as it is nothing to do with me. Spirituality is totally different to religion and, yes, there is a strong spiritual overlay to my work.

A good deal of research was carried out in the early part of the twentieth century; prior to that, those in the West didn't really think about it and those in the East just took it for granted.

It is impossible to talk about reincarnation research without mentioning the work of Dr Ian Stevenson (1918 – 2007). He founded what was originally called the *Division of Personality Studies*, now called the *Division of Perceptual Studies*, at the University of Virginia School of Medicine in 1967. He served as Chairman of the Department of Psychiatry at the university and was honoured as the Carlson Professor of Psychiatry there too. So he was a highly experienced and very well-respected academic.

A medical doctor and a psychiatrist who became disillusioned with psychoanalysis, he was the first person to approach research into children who remember past lives using methods that were as empirical and scientific as they could be. Starting in 1961 and for the next forty years, he and his team researched more than two thousand cases, primarily in Asia where the concept is accepted. His methodology was to the highest of standards, bearing in mind he was applying scientific principles to areas which, at that time, were ignored by other researchers.

Stevenson's work started with children who reported memories of a past life, believing that they were unlikely to make up such stories. He would gather as much information as possible from the child about their previous life, including details of their family, where they lived, what the home looked like, how they died and so on. This was to build as full a picture as possible. Then he would take the child with their current parents to the place the child claimed to have lived and assess the accuracy of the child's descriptions.

Did the child recognise the town or village and the house? Could he or she identify the other family members and provide personal information about them? Could that family confirm those details, including how the child had died?

In 2018, Dr Ian Stevenson's successor at the University of Virginia, Dr Jim Tucker, stated that Stevenson and his team compiled over two and a half thousand childhood past life memory cases. In 1,567 of those cases, the past life personality was identified through research. In another 150 cases, the past life personality had been 'tentatively' identified. That's a very large percentage of successful hits.

His research revealed some interesting principles that have been confirmed by later studies. For instance, personality traits and habits seem to persist from one incarnation to another and physical features can be very similar too. There are often identical birthmarks from one lifetime to the next; or, if there was death by, say, a stabbing or shooting, there could be a birthmark at exactly that point on the body in the next incarnation. Stevenson estimated that gender stayed the same in around ninety per cent of cases and hypothesised that when gender change does occur, this might create issues around gender identity.

Later in his career, Stevenson researched European reincarnation cases in an attempt to overcome resistance to the concept. His 2003 book *European Cases of the Reincarnation Type* contains eight cases that had not been previously investigated from the first third of the twentieth century, twenty-one cases from the second half of the century that were independently investigated, and seven cases of vivid or recurring dreams. All are reported not quite as a scientific report but still sticking to academic criteria.[5]

'*The writings of most modern scientists,*' he wrote, '*offer no solution to the seeming injustice of birth defects and other inequalities at birth. Instead they depict an exclusively material existence ending in extinction at death. Unsatisfied with this, many human beings – perhaps especially in modern Europe – continue to search for some meaning to life that transcends their own present existence.*

'*Reincarnation offers hope of a life after death; and it offers a possibility of our eventually understanding the causes of our suffering. These offerings* [that is, the case studies he presents in the book] *do not make it true; only evidence can show whether it is or is not true. They may, however, account for the increasing attractiveness of the belief in reincarnation.*'

His contribution to the field of reincarnation study is enormous. He opened many doors and paved the way for both researchers and therapists to follow in his footsteps and his many papers and books serve as fascinating reference material for anyone who wishes to know more about the subject.

Dr Jim Tucker worked with Dr Ian Stevenson for a number of years and took over the reins at the University of Virginia in 2014. He holds degrees in psychology and medicine, and has considerable

---

[5] McFarland & Co.

experience in his chosen field of psychiatry with children, adolescents and adults. The prime focus of his work has been with children in America and he brings the same rigorous methodology that Dr Ian Stevenson applied in those pioneering days. Dr Tucker has developed a method of evaluating cases that he calls 'The Strength of Case Scale', to ensure consistency and scientific principles are applied to all investigations. He has written several books, including *Life before Life: A Scientific Investigation of Children's Memories of Previous Lives*[6] and *Before: Children's Memories of Previous Lives*[7].

Roy Stemman started researching 'all things paranormal' in his teenage years and applies the analytical approach of an investigative journalist to the field of reincarnation. He researches the researchers, if you will, and the therapists too. Roy has travelled around the world investigating claims, meeting and working with other eminent figures in the world of reincarnation studies as well as working on his own cases. His many books include *One Soul: Many Lives*[8] and, previously mentioned, *The Big Book of Reincarnation*, which bring together considerable research and fascinating stories from his own travels and those of others.

Reincarnation is a vast field and I have only raked the surface here. After all, this is not an academic textbook but rather one that will give some useful background information to those who have never looked at the subject before, and will provide stories from my own case files to show reincarnation in action, as past life regression for healing.

---

[6] Piatkus (2009)
[7] St. Martin's Essentials (2021)
[8] Ulysses Press (2005)

CHAPTER 7

Slavery

There are moments in the history of any country that instil pride and there are periods that show another side. Slavery was far more widely spread than our contemporary media would have us believe. It was not just dreadful white people rounding up black people and using them as slaves in their own country or transporting them around the world to be sold for profit. White people trafficked white people and black people trafficked black people too and, unfortunately, still do.

    The trauma of slavery is one that inevitably would burn into the soul and carry through lifetimes. I work with clients of all shapes and sizes, colours and creeds. To me, they are all the same, people who have taken the brave step to seek help in resolving an issue that is holding them back in this lifetime. Only in the following two stories does the colour of the client matter, which is why it is mentioned: both ladies were black, totally unknown to each other, but with striking similarities in their stories.

Ella came to see me when she was in her early sixties. A highly intelligent career woman, she explained that the time had come for her to address the various "niggles", as she called them, that had been building up inside her. She had experienced a turbulent upbringing within her extended family and that pattern showed in her own life as unhealthy relationships and not being able 'to speak up'.

She told me about when she was at school studying for her A Levels. She had put her hand up in class to answer a question and when the teacher turned to her she found she couldn't speak, such had been the programming in her earlier life. Managing to overcome that, she went on to forge a very successful career in her chosen profession. And yet…

"There's something," she said, "that needs to come out and I can't do it on my own."

As is often the way with high achievers, we found it was hard for her to relax in our early sessions but it became easier when she was more comfortable with the process. Then she allowed herself to sink into a deep state of relaxation and found the door that she had chosen.

We met Annie, a girl of fourteen who told me she was wearing a long skirt with a small print and a nice top in a pale yellow colour. Annie was indoors and looking out of the window where she could see that it was very nice weather and there were children playing in the distance, although she didn't know who they were. She said that it was a big house but it wasn't hers. I asked Annie how she was feeling and she told me that she wished she could be outside, playing like the other children. When I asked what was preventing her from doing just that, she replied, "I've got things to do, chores, cleaning. I've got dark skin…" Then I asked Annie about her family.

"I don't remember my family. I've been at this house for a very long time now, I can't remember anywhere else." She didn't know the name of the house or of the family who owned it, but she called them "Massah", so I asked about the owners of that big house. "The owner man is middle-aged and medium build. He's white. He wears some kind of wig and a red tunic with gold braiding and has stockings on his legs. I can't see his wife."

She explained that she worked at the house doing cleaning, a lot of cleaning, and she was not aware of any other people working there. The 'owner man' seemed all right to work for, not unkind to Annie as long as she did her work as he expected. What happened if the work was not done? Ella gave a big sigh, then Annie answered, "The work is always done."

I next met Annie some six years later when she was twenty and had a baby at her breast. I encouraged her to tell me the story, asking how she felt about having a baby and who the father was.

"I don't feel happy," she replied, "I just feel neutral. I don't know who the father is, it might be Massah, I don't know. It's a baby boy and he has lighter skin than me and he has Massah's face, so I must have had sex with him…" Was Massah happy that she had given birth to a baby boy? "I don't know, I'm not allowed to see him."

Annie explained that she was no longer in the big house but in a much smaller property within the grounds. She was not sure if she was still working for Massah. The baby had been born some three months before and was called Bruce, although Annie couldn't tell me who chose that name. She said she could not remember the birth but both she and Bruce were healthy. It seemed that she had drawn a veil of forgetfulness over the entire episode of having sex – most probably against her will – of the pregnancy and the birth, and was not really sure what was going on. I asked if her life would change now that she had a baby.

"I feel there might be prospects now, through the baby," Annie told me. "His lighter skin is his passport that might help his mother." She said that even though she had not seen Massah since the baby was born, she felt sure he was aware of the situation and was looking after her, providing accommodation and food and so on. By the time Annie was about thirty-eight, Bruce was eighteen and she was a very proud Mum.

"He looks good, he's got a tricorn hat on and he's in some sort of uniform, like he's going somewhere but not to fight."

It was clear to Annie that Bruce's father, the 'owner man', had been providing for them over the years, including an education for Bruce. Annie had only seen Massah a few times over the years yet he seemed quite pleased with his son's progress. I asked Annie to tell me more about Bruce.

"He went to school here on the island where the big house is. It's called Hispaniola. And now he is off to study in England and he's happy at the thought of leaving here. He is wearing the uniform of the white people, it looks military but it's not... I'm quite glad he's going, but I feel sad too."

Annie then explained that she'd had another child, a daughter called Sorcha who was ten years-old. Sorcha's father was not Massah. "Her skin is too dark, more like mine. I don't think she's mixed and I haven't been sleeping with Massah." Eventually Annie reached the conclusion that Sorcha's father was Ben, who had married Annie after the baby was born. Ben was a builder, a good man, who knew and accepted that Massah was Bruce's father. "Generally I'm comfortable," said Annie. "I've lived above average."

In the next chapter of her life, Annie was in her early fifties. Ben had vanished from her life; as far as she knew he was not dead but she had no idea where he was. "As long as I have my daughter, I'm okay, he can go," she said. She explained that Sorcha was a good girl and they were close. Sorcha was now about eighteen and had received an education, albeit not as good as Bruce's. Bruce was still abroad and regularly sent her money. He was about thirty and his work was "something to do with ships" although she didn't know where in the world he was. Massah seems to have faded from the picture.

At the end of her life, Annie was about seventy years-old. She was at her home with both Bruce and Sorcha by her side. Asked to review her life, she said, "I feel I've done alright. I feel content that the children turned out well." Her passing thought was, "I left my children in a good place." The soul seemed content with that lifetime too. "It was a life well spent. She learned how to progress, she learned diplomacy and patience." The goals for this current life were to learn how to be herself, to be braver and more resilient. The main obstacle would be oppression.

The healing work done around that lifetime allowed Ella to release a lot of the trauma in this lifetime regarding family dynamics and she said it all made a lot of sense to her.

This was a peaceful life compared to many of the others in this book, and showed that not all slave owners were cruel and heartless. Yes, Massah undoubtedly took advantage of Annie and raped her, that seemed to have been par for the course, an accepted privilege. But to his credit, and no doubt because the resulting child was a boy with pale enough skin for him to pass as white, Massah took care of mother and child from a distance.

Young and naïve thought she was, Annie realised that a boy child with pale skin was not only her son's passport to freedom but hers too. Hispaniola is the second largest island of the West Indies, in the Caribbean. Today it is made up of Haiti and the Dominican Republic. Christopher Columbus landed there in 1492 and named it La Isla Española. The island produces many crops that would certainly have attracted the attention of merchants and businessmen, including tobacco, cacao, coffee and sugarcane, and slave ownership would have been common.

Nicola came to see me in her mid-forties. Her job in healthcare meant she was always looking after other people and never looking after herself. Her emotional batteries were flat. She told me that she suffered from a lack of self-confidence. As for men, a string of failed relationships had led her to say, "Never again," and she was spiritually aware enough to know that such a phrase probably had its roots somewhere else. Indeed it did.

Nicola quickly and easily sank into a deep state of relaxation and found the door that would lead her to the past life she needed to explore. We met a young lady called Angeline who told me she was around twenty years-old. She was barefoot, wearing a long skirt and a white blouse. Angeline said she was outdoors in a tropical place, warm with lots of greenery and quite swampy. She explained that she was alone and was a slave working on a sugar cane plantation in Jamaica for a woman she called 'the White Witch'.

Angeline was black, had been a slave all her life and could not recall having parents. She said she mainly worked in the big house on the plantation, cooking, cleaning and washing clothes. The White Witch was not an easy woman; she scared Angeline, there were too many rules, too many threats. I asked Angeline if she had a husband or a boyfriend and she laughed.

"Ha! No. I have no husband, no lover, no boyfriend. The White Witch will pick a husband for me with her overseer." On the couch, Nicola was moving about and showing signs of discomfort. I asked Angeline to tell me about life there on the plantation, to tell me more about the White Witch and the overseer. "The young women are raped in order to have babies," she explained. "The overseers are white and they choose the young black slaves." She herself had not yet had a baby but the rape had started recently with one particular overseer and she knew she was pregnant. The White Witch didn't care about that, the work in the big house still had to be done. Other slave women didn't want to get involved because they were all scared of the White Witch.

Angeline gave birth to a baby girl in a very basic shack somewhere on the plantation and there was an older woman, also a slave, there with her. The baby had been born about a week earlier and she was still bleeding, but otherwise she was fine and the baby, whom she called Sarah, was also healthy. The father had seen the baby and had already said that he wanted more.

"He's not going to marry me," Angeline said, with bitterness in her voice, "but he wants more babies. He won't look after me, he just wants me to produce more babies."

I invited Angeline to move forward in that lifetime to the next important event, and now she was very happy. "The overseer is dead!" she told me. "There was an accident on the plantation and he's dead. I'm free!"

Sarah had been given away, as had two other baby girls she had given birth to, all by the same man. The only child she was allowed to keep was a boy who was then aged ten and who was living with another family. She had no idea where the girls had gone except that it was into a life of slavery. She explained that she still worked at the big house but now that her children's father was dead, she could rest.

"I'm relieved that he's dead," she said. "I am so happy that he is dead. He didn't look after me or any of his children, he was a horrible man."

Ten years later, Angeline had more good news. Her son was free. He was now aged twenty and there had been many changes at the plantation. The White Witch had gone and for the last five years a new white man had been in charge.

"I work for him," Angeline told me. "He's fair and he is starting to free all of the slaves. My son is now free! He has some land but it is not close by. I'll stay here in the big house. He doesn't know I'm his mother, I won't tell him… I'm too old for children now, there's no trouble from other men."

At the end of her life, Angeline was in bed in her home, a small shack on the plantation estate. A friend was with her and she said it was "Hot, hot, hot." I asked her to look back over her life and say what she made of it. "I'm bitter and I'm angry—" she almost spat out the words, "—because it was a wasted life. I was used and I was abused by the White Witch and by that overseer." Her passing thought was, "Never again."

The soul said in its review that the lessons were sacrifice, independence and strength. "There was too much pain," I was told. "She loved her babies but she had to give them up." The lessons for this current lifetime were to learn to love men again, to trust, to forgive and to move on. The advice was, "Let it go."

Nicola was certainly overweight when she came to see me and I asked the soul if that excess weight had anything to do with her lifetime as Angeline. The answer was positive, saying that, "The excess weight is protecting her from that fear. It will be hard for her to let it go but she has to do that. She has to be prepared to let it go."

Nicola's first remark when she had come back from the state of relaxation was very revealing.

"Now I know why I won't go out with white men," she said. "I've often tried but something always held me back, I would have a feeling in my stomach. Now I know why!"

Angeline's story resonated deeply with Nicola and she felt the same range of emotions in the here and now that Angeline had on her death bed – bitterness and anger at her treatment by the overseer – mixed with sadness that she had to give up her babies and was denied a loving relationship of her own. The trauma of that lifetime had clearly been carried over into this one, and the healing that was done around it allowed Nicola to start a clean sheet when it came to forming healthy relationships with men, black or white.

Jamaica, an island in the Caribbean, was discovered by Christopher Columbus on his voyage to the New World and was colonised by the Spanish in 1509, tempted by Columbus' descriptions of "Plentiful food and new exotic crops". It proved to be a very useful restocking stop-off point for the rest of the Caribbean. The British conquered the island in 1655, although it was bitterly disputed for years after that. When the Spanish realised that they had been defeated, they released livestock and slaves and told the slaves they could kill the British with impunity. In Angeline's story, she only referred to the White Witch and the white overseer. She didn't say they were English, so they could well have been Spanish.

After the Battle of Sedgemoor in July, 1685, in Somerset, where a revolt by the Duke of Monmouth was quashed, many of the defeated rebels were hanged or transported to distant colonies, including Jamaica. On board the ship *Jamaica Merchant* was one William Rowe. When I asked Angeline about the big house on the plantation, she couldn't tell me the name but she did say what I took to be "Rose Hoar." Having heard her story, could it be that William Rowe, a rebel soldier from the West of England, became an overseer alongside the White Witch and that Angeline found herself called "Rowe's Whore"?

It's not only women who were enslaved, of course, and this account tells of one young native boy who, whilst not exactly a slave, became perhaps a bit too friendly with invading forces, long ago and far away.

Dave was about fifty when he came to see me. A sensitive man on his own spiritual journey, he was keen to explore all avenues in the search for his 'true self'. There were issues around relationships and family and he told me that he felt a bit lost, somehow the odd one out. He went to regular meditation classes and was therefore familiar with relaxation techniques, so he found the doorway to a past life easily.

A young boy said he was five years-old but was not able to tell me his name. He was on a beach, it was warm and sunny and he was just admiring the view. He clearly knew the place well and pointed out two large rocks just off the shore which made it dangerous for swimming or for navigating a boat. The boy said he was part of a tribe that lived inland from the beach, in forest huts. Everything was all right with the tribe, there was food, they could fish and there was no sickness. Yet there was a sense of foreboding. The elders of the tribe had warned of danger from the sea and they had done ceremonies on the beach.

"We hope the rocks will keep us safe," said the boy.

I next found him six years later when strangers had indeed arrived on ships. There had not been any battle but these strangers had certainly caused a stir and there was considerable suspicion among the tribe. The boy was curious, in awe of these white men who wore uniforms and spoke a different language. There was a lot of noise and hustle and bustle as supplies were unloaded for the strangers while they set up camp. There were crates and barrels and sacks of provisions, and lots of these white people.

The boy told me that he'd met one of these strangers who was wearing a uniform. He did not know his name but called him "Officer." Officer was a young man who was a sort of botanist and observer, not really like the others, and he seemed genuinely interested in everything around him, including the boy.

"I'm very cautious," explained the boy. "I want to show him all sorts of things but the tribe… they don't like it, they don't trust the strangers. They say we will all become slaves."

Just over a decade later the strangers are still there, they seem to have established a base and have settled in for a long stay. The boy is confused.

"It seems I'm the one that allowed them to infiltrate. I'm like a spy, I'm being manipulated by the visitors. I sort of recognise what's going on but I don't want to believe it… I'm sat next to Officer and other visitors, fraternising with the enemy. I have given away secrets of our tribe, I've sold my soul to the visitors. I was blinded by what they brought here and gave me, their technology, alcohol…"

It was clear that the boy – now a young man although I shall continue to call him the boy – was understanding the implications of what he and a few others in his tribe had been doing. He had taken the strangers to sources of fresh water, shown them medicinal plants and given away secrets of the tribe. In return the strangers let him sit at the same table when they had their meals, plied him with alcohol and gave him trinkets.

"I have been domesticated like an animal," the boy said. "I have given away the knowledge of the tribe and I am nothing more than a tame animal." He was deeply troubled. "This has been coming since I was five years-old," he told me. "Look at me now. I'm sad and I'm lonely. I have given up my birthright. I should not have helped them. I'm lost. I'm not one of them, and never will be, and yet now I am not welcome in my tribe either… Officer and the other visitors, they treat me all right, but I'm a joke, I see that now. I'm completely separate, they laugh at me. I'm sat on a rock in my tribal dress and I am being mocked. I don't have the right to wear it. I have a spear but it doesn't matter. They have guns. I am no threat to them, I'm just a silly black man in a ridiculous outfit."

By the time he was thirty-six, the boy seemed to have regained some equilibrium about the situation.

"I am not in a drunken stupor anymore," he said, "and I have regained some of my self-worth. I know who I am. I am wearing my full ceremonial dress, it's my birthright to wear it and I wear it with pride." I was encouraged to hear this, but then he went on, "I'm standing right on the edge of a high rock and I am about to jump off. I am hanging on to the belief that somehow I helped to bring understanding between the visitors and my tribe. I feel I was abandoned by my tribe. How long have I been in this no-man's-land? Nobody knows I am doing this and I don't care. I've found some kind of inner strength and self-respect. I feel some raw power, I've painted my body and I'm screaming to the gods. There is anger in me, not at humans but at the gods, I want to fight the gods. I'm jumping because I want to meet the gods and wage war against them."

And jump he did. His passing thought was, "I've reclaimed my power."

The soul, in reviewing that life, explained that it had been a lesson in regaining personal power. There is power in belonging to a tribe, of being part of something larger, but the strongest power is that inside, listening to the voice of the soul. The lesson for this current lifetime is not to be a chameleon, changing colours to suit the situation.

"He will be placed in a number of situations," the soul explained, "that will challenge him to be his true self. He will have to extract himself from those challenging him so he will find who he really is. He will also be placed into situations that may be comfortable but are not moving him forward.

"He has to learn to reclaim his true self without having to jump off a cliff. There will be suffering and there will be confrontation, it will not always be easy but it can lead to a breakthrough. Nobody has created a better existence by doing nothing." And the advice was encouraging. "Something will come. Don't be scared of it, look forward to it. Whatever you are now, you are just hiding in the shadows and the true you needs to come into the light."

When he came back from his past life journey, Dave was bewildered more than anything else by the clarity and intensity of the experience.

"I felt I was an aborigine in Australia," he told me. "I don't know how I know that, I just felt it to be true." His ancestors had spent generations in Australia so there was a link there, but he had not delved into the history of the indigenous people. He could associate with the boy's curiosity about the newcomers and wanting to know more, but also with that sense of giving too much away to please others and, in doing so, risking his bedrock and foundation.

"I do sometimes have problems knowing who I am meant to be at any given time," he admitted, "when actually I should just be me, shouldn't I?"

CHAPTER 8

Wives and Husbands

Many years ago I took part in a workshop led by Roger Woolger. We were working in pairs, taking it in turn to find a past life and report back on it. The lady I was working with had her turn, then it was mine and I duly found a past life in the Middle Ages in central Europe.

I was the daughter of a wealthy merchant, in love with someone my father considered to be 'not good enough' for me. One evening, my lover came for me and we escaped, the two of us on his horse. We rode away from the town, all the way through a big forest and out the other side. There, eventually, we built a little wooden cabin and had a very quiet life. He died first and I buried him in the garden.

"I wonder who will bury me?" I thought.

As I was relating this to my partner, Roger came to check on us and I reported the life I had found. Roger Woolger was tall and dark-haired with a twinkle in his eye, an absolute charmer as well as a brilliant researcher, teacher and therapist. He looked at me.

"No, no, no!" he roared. "I don't want peaceful lives. I want drama, I want trauma! Go back and find another life."

Well, no, not all our lives have been full of violence or trauma. We have all had lives that were happy and joyful or quiet and peaceful. The point is this: just as we only go to the dentist when we have toothache, people only come to see me, or any other therapist, when they have issues to be resolved. And it is almost always the case that the past lives that have left an imprint or impression on the soul are those that involved a serious element of trauma.

When things are going smoothly and all is well, the soul is happy and that joy is registered; but it does not leave the deep imprint that trauma does. In the same way, of course, even in this current lifetime, we don't learn life lessons when everything is going well. We learn from the crises, from those times when our world falls around our ears and we have to pick ourselves up and sort ourselves out.

Over the years, I would say about two-thirds of my clients have been women and one-third men, with ages ranging from mid-twenties to a gentleman who celebrated his eightieth birthday while we were working together. The stories in this chapter are about wives who were killed by their husbands in one way or another and it's easy to see that this would certainly count as trauma and would leave an imprint on the soul. What is most interesting, though, is the varying ways in which it shows up in this lifetime and how it impacts the here and now.

Janet came to see me when she was in her mid-thirties, suffering from anxiety and relationship issues. She went nicely into a deep state of relaxation and found the door to the past life that her unconscious, or higher self, had chosen.

There we met Beth, a young lady in her twenties. She told me she was wearing hessian-type boots, a long dress and a long apron, saying, "I'm all covered up." Her mousy blonde hair was braided and tied up in a bonnet. Beth explained that she was in her home, a log cabin with a fire burning in the hearth. She had a husband and two young children, a boy aged two and a girl aged four, although she could not tell me their names. I asked for more information about her husband.

"He wears black and white – a white shirt and white socks, with black trousers, a black jacket and black shoes. He sometimes has a beard."

I asked Beth if she knew what year it was. Janet heaved a big sigh and Beth said, "A very long time ago, maybe the 1500s." She explained it was almost wintertime and it was cold and raining. The children were there at home, her husband would get home in the dark.

"It's very restrictive around here," she said, and I asked her to explain what she meant by that. "We are not allowed to think or feel, we have to believe what they want you to believe." Who were "they"? "The people who run the town, my husband works for them. I don't like them, they own and control the town. We have to go to church. We have to behave. We have to be good and nice. In the church, we have to do God's work. God is watching and we will be punished if we don't do what He says. We will burn in Hell."

Beth explained that she was not originally part of this group, she'd only joined five years earlier when she married her husband.

"He has to be part of the group like his parents. My parents were not part of it. I didn't know anything about the group, I just loved my husband. He's powerful, he's high up in the group, like a justice, so he can do what he likes.

"My husband sometimes treats me well and sometimes not, he shouts. He hit me once when people were watching because the man is meant to be strong and dominant to keep the woman in line. He treats the children all right, he plays with them when he can. There is conflict within him between who he has to be and who he really wants to be. He's not really that hard."

I asked about Beth's life before she joined the group.

"My life was free and loving. I would spend lots of time in the woods. There was lots of dancing. There's no dancing allowed in the group, but my husband and my children and I dance."

I caught up with Beth a few years later when her daughter was aged eight. She was facing death.

"The elders of the group saw me dancing in the woods. I was just walking through the trees, having a little dance. They caught me, dragged me back to the town and beat me. The elders accused me of putting a spell on the town, they said it was my fault that they were having money and food problems. I had brought it upon them. Now they are going to burn me alive… it's what they do… my poor husband is terrified. If he doesn't go along with it, the elders will take the children.

"The elders don't know but when I was tied to the stake, before they lit the fire, my husband shot me through the heart to save me suffering. He had to protect the children. My life was short, wasn't it? But that's all right, it was all right." Her passing thoughts were of, "His faith, the sadness, his love, my anger…"

When I asked the soul for its review of that life, it said it was not good having to hide her true self. The life was unsettling and clearly it did not like the conflict. There was a pause and then the soul continued that conflict and expectations were put upon Beth to force her to conform, so the challenge was to know her true self.

This was followed by a conversation with the soul, asking questions on behalf of Janet which provided considerable understanding and insight for Janet and her child. That part of the session was at a deep soul level and was very emotional for Janet, but it helped her enormously. Her feedback on the session was that Beth knew who she was and what she was doing. She was not afraid of dying, it was part of her journey. The real healing here was the connection that was made between Janet and her soul, experiencing that vast energy, the wisdom and compassion that enveloped her.

At an historical level, Beth seemed accurately to be describing the Puritan movement, which grew within the Church of England in the late sixteenth century. The Puritans were religious reformers who felt that the Church of England had grown to be too similar to the Roman Catholic Church; they wanted to take things back to strict observance of the Bible, with none of the trimmings or ceremonies. The movement had started in the 1530s when Henry VIII broke away from Rome. Many Puritans left England in the early 1600s, some to Holland and many more to America, to New England. The strictures of their life and outlook would match very closely what Beth described, also the typical clothing, both for herself and her husband.

When I work with a client I remind them that, in the past life, all of their senses will be active: they will be able to hear, see, touch, taste and feel all that is around them. Sometimes I nudge them to do just that by asking, "What can you smell there in the market place?" or "How do you feel in your wedding dress?" or "What can you hear there in the jungle?" And it always worked that way – until I met Ally.

Ally was a bright and bubbly young lady in her mid-thirties, her outgoing front masking issues around self-worth and self-confidence, which had more recently developed into severe anxiety. There were various emotional issues challenging her when we met, and we had made a good start at 'peeling the emotional onion' to strip away the layers of 'stuff' that had built up over the years. By the time we reached this past life session, therefore, Ally was comfortable with the process of allowing herself to go into a deep state of relaxation and she easily found the door that she wanted to go through into her chosen past life.

This is where I discovered an interesting situation, the only time I have come across it: the person we met in the past life was unable to speak! How would I get answers from them if they were not able to verbalise what they wanted to tell me?

Well, there was a three-fold solution: my intuition, my pendulum and blinking. Even when a client has their eyes closed, they can blink, and it can be a slight movement or a real screwing up of the eyes. It was a technique that I had rarely used, but then this was very rare case. I explained to the past life character how it would work – one clear blink for 'Yes' and two clear blinks for 'No'. Did they understand? There was one clear blink so that was a good start.

Are you a man? Two clear blinks. Are you a woman? One clear blink. The system seemed to be working. So even though this is a short story in itself, it took a lot of time and effort to put together the pieces of the puzzle, going back and double-checking answers, asking the same thing in different ways and so on to make sure that I was getting the right messages.

There was no way I could easily find the lady's name with this method so I shall call her Marion. Marion 'told' me that she was forty years-old. She was in Europe and it was the 1300s. She was a princess and this was her wedding day. Her father the king had arranged the marriage, but she was very happy nonetheless. Her husband-to-be was a younger man, the king of lands that her father had recently conquered, thus the marriage was designed to bring the lands together for future generations.

The festivities were in the open air and lots of people had gathered to celebrate the occasion. I let the story unfold in its own time as this was clearly not one to be rushed, and the fact that we first met Marion on her wedding day indicated that this was where the action was, as it were. And so it proved. Marion did not get to enjoy new-found happiness for long.

The very next day, her new husband killed her by a mixture of stabbing and strangulation. The younger man, having been conquered in battle, took his revenge on the king by brutally killing his daughter. He could not face a life with an older woman who could not speak; for him, that was as humiliating as defeat in battle.

So he murdered her, knowing that he himself would then face death yet perhaps feeling it would be a more honourable end.

I asked Marion to tell me more about her life and a picture slowly emerged. She had never been able to speak and this had, perhaps inevitably in those days, distanced her from her siblings and her parents. In her younger days she'd had a lover, the man who took care of the horses at her father's palace. Through spending time with her lover in the stables, Marion discovered that she had an affinity with the animals, she could communicate with them and they with her. She'd also had a daughter with her lover, and it was this daughter who found Marion's body lying in a pool of blood, the rope still around her neck.

There was considerable healing work done for Marion and the soul around the trauma of that death and the other challenges of that lifetime, including not being able to communicate.

When I brought Ally back from that deep state of relaxation, she was astounded at what we had found. Marion's beautiful gift of being able to communicate with horses had been carried forward to this lifetime, but so had her challenge of not being able to speak. In this lifetime, this had translated into Ally's reticence to 'speak her truth', to tell people how good she was at what she did, and it manifested in her lack of self-confidence and self-worth. After all, Marion had been cast aside and largely ignored by her own family and the only attention she received was from the man who worked with the horses.

Ally told me that her mother had taken her own life and it was Ally who had found the body, a trauma with clear echoes of Marion's daughter finding her body when she had been killed by her new husband.

"So many things made sense to me," she said at our next session, "and have been falling into place since last time. I have been sleeping really well and I feel much more energetically and spiritually aware now."

Sometimes a past life story can be long and detailed, with many stops along the way from the point of first meeting the character to their death. A full picture is built of a life well lived, or not, and we gain fascinating insights into the life and times of that period along the way. Sometimes the past life story is short and not-so-sweet. We may, as with Marion above, join the story at the crucial point, in her case when she was already forty years old. Or we may find a young life cut short for any number of reasons, in any number of ways.

Georgia was nudging fifty when she came to see me, a very sensitive lady who had had a number of spiritual experiences in her life, and it was that aspect of my work that attracted her to me. There were a number of issues in her life that she was struggling to make sense of, to put in a wider context, and she hoped that a past life session might shed light on some of them, especially relationships. Having done meditation and yoga practice, Georgia went easily into a deep state of relaxation and soon found the door she wanted to go through.

There we found a young lady who introduced herself as Jenny, giving her age as "around eighteen or twenty-four". Jenny explained that she was in in prison, saying, "It's a dark place, everything around me is black." I asked what she had done wrong, why she found herself in prison.

"I've done nothing wrong," she said, quietly. "They say I'm not a good wife, I'm not doing what's expected of me. I'm not loyal. People say I'm a bad wife but I just want to be myself. My husband is a tyrant, I don't want to be close to him at all, I push him away." I asked Jenny to tell me more about her husband. "His name is John, he's at least thirty, probably more. Ha! Nobody would be in love with him. I had to marry him, my parents made me do it. My parents are poor and John rules the place, but he's not a nice man… he's raped me lots of times, and now he's put me in prison. He's got someone else now anyway.

"I've been in prison a few months now, I suppose, I don't really know. I can't see anyone else but I know there are other people here – and rats, lots of rats. The place is damp, it stinks. It's in a big castle somewhere but I don't know where…"

When I next met Jenny, she was still in that same prison.

"I don't know how old I am now, I don't know how long I've been in prison, I would guess years by now. I'm going to die, I'm very ill, something is eating me, probably the rats. I've got a headache too… I can't be angry anymore, I don't have any strength left."

At the end of her life, Jenny was moved to a place next to the prison and left there to die.

"I don't know what I'm dying of," she told me. "I just know I'm dying, this is where they leave people to die and I am all alone, there's nobody here with me." I asked her to look back over her life and say what she made of it. "Life? What life? I think nothing about my life," she wheezed. Her passing thought was, "I don't know where I'm going… I'm afraid, I'm sad…"

The soul's review of that lifetime was that it was empty and sad. When preparing for this current lifetime, then, I was told that the lessons were to stay focused and to follow the path regardless. The challenges were to trust oneself and others, even though there would be rejection.

"Look at your feet and keep on your path. Regardless of who they are, they are there to help you. They are not bad people, they are there to help you to find your way, to stick to your path, despite the challenges."

The feelings of being punished even though she had done nothing wrong resonated strongly with Georgia, as did the sense of not being free to do what she wanted to do. There had been conflict with her partner around these very points and, even though Georgia did not call her partner a tyrant, she made it clear that he liked to rule the roost.

Jenny's emotions after being in prison for so long, "I can't be angry anymore, I don't have any strength left," were very familiar to Georgia. She understood, though, that her partner and others in her family circle were part of her soul group, not always to be kind and loving but to test her to the limits she had set herself for this lifetime, and to challenge her to achieve the goal of finding her pathway and sticking to it.

At the next session, Georgia told me she had gone deep inside to find answers. A big cloud had lifted, allowing her to see situations much more clearly. She had allowed herself to be put in a position that echoed Jenny's, having to choose between stagnating in a relationship that was stifling, yet seen as 'acceptable', or breaking free of the metaphorical prison to follow her own path.

She had given herself permission to acknowledge the truth of the situation and to allow the inevitable process to unfold.

Hasn't every woman dreamed of a knight in shining armour coming to rescue her from a life of drudgery, to sweep her off…? And how many women have thought that they'd found their Prince Charming who would love and cherish them for ever, only to have that illusion shattered? They say that love is a burning flame. So it was for Nanda, but not quite in the way she would have hoped.

Maureen was a career woman in her mid-forties when she came to see me with a familiar mix of issues on her shopping list: anxiety, over-eating and, most of all, relationships. She told me she had been with her current partner for five years or more although her previous partner was still at the back of her mind; and every time there was an argument, the previous partner would come into the picture. I did a lot of work with Maureen over the course of a year or so and, as each emotional issue was addressed, so I could almost see her breathing more easily, coming back to her true self and becoming clearer at physical, mental and emotional levels. Her past life story was not the prettiest, but it brought her a number of insights and a deeper level of understanding.

Through the door to a past life, I met a young lady called Nanda. She told me was indoors, she was barefoot, and there were cool stones under her feet. She gave her age as mid-twenties. There was no light but she could make out an old wooden desk and a chair. There was a window with no glass, high up. She said it felt like a castle and smelled like a cellar.

Nanda said she could make out a door, "It's like in an old, enchanted tower", but that she was scared to open it and thought maybe she was locked in there. I suggested to Nanda that maybe she was not locked in, and the door might open if she tried it. It did, and she found herself in a long corridor with stone slabs on the floor and thickly hewn stone walls. As she walked further, there were candle holders on the walls with flickering candles giving more light. The corridor got wider and then stairs led up to another door. When she opened that one, she found herself in a room of a castle with a fire blazing in the big ornate fireplace. There was a deep red, velvety sofa and a footstool, and a table with a pewter decanter on it.

"I don't know what I'm doing here," commented Nanda. "Servants are asking if I would like some wine and some food… they are treating me very well, as if I am a lady… I get the sense that I am waiting for someone…"

I caught up with Nanda again a little while later. She was still in the castle but now her wait was over.

"He is just like Prince Charming from the fairy tales," said Nanda. "He is a prince and this is his castle. He hugs me and he kisses me and he is telling me that he loves me… but I know there is something he is not telling me." There was a pause before she continued, "He's marrying someone else. I cannot be his wife because I'm not a princess, I'm not respectable enough… I have loved him for a long time. I don't know what to feel, I'm hurt, I'm upset, confused…"

Nanda was clearly emotional, and tears were trickling down Maureen's cheek at this point. I just held the space and allowed the story to move on in its own time. I found Nanda in another part of the castle.

"Guards are taking me to somewhere else in the castle, it's a room with stone floors and stone walls but there is a big fire in the middle of the room…" Her voice faded as she realised what was to come. "I'm scared, I don't want to stay here, this is like a witch hunt but I'm not a witch. I'm pregnant, I'm carrying the prince's baby… is that why he wants rid of me? He told me he loved me and now he is going to let me burn… I don't understand, I love him… the fire, the flames…"

The soul was not altogether happy about what was in store for Maureen's current lifetime.

"I am not allowed to take revenge, I mustn't do that. I need to be good, nice, follow the rules and follow a plan. It sounds like a military operation and I don't want to do that! I like to be happy and relaxed but I have to follow the rules. I need to find a cause and fight for it. I need to be the heroine who changes something. There will be many challenges, it's going to be a hard life and I'm not sure I can live up to all these expectations. It's too much, I can't save the world on my own."

Yet the advice to Maureen was, "Don't feel so overwhelmed. You are allowed to be happy and you don't have to save the world all by yourself, just do what you can. Relax."

Maureen was quite shocked, when she came back from her journey, at how real it had all been. She told me that she had been able to feel the stone walls, the velvety sofa and the heat of the fire.

"But," she said, "I don't remember much after the initial heat of the fire."

No, because I moved her through the point of death in that lifetime. There is nothing to be gained in having someone relive every minute of such a long and painful death. The emotions were clear, and they were cleared there, at their source, as part of the healing process.

At the next session, Maureen said that the processing of the past life experience had been emotional but insightful. She understood more clearly how she had been torn between her current partner and her previous one, and how this was not allowing her to move forward or be happy. The Prince Charming who sent her to her death was, indeed, her previous partner. And, at another level, she could also see that everything that needed to go up in flames was her present 'stuff'.

Sometimes these past lives don't have to have full historical chapter and verse. The stories that unfold are just what is needed to provide the insights needed to allow the client to understand themselves better, to take on board the soul's advice and to move on.

CHAPTER 9

Health of Body and Mind

Sometimes the link between a past life and an issue in this life is blatantly obvious, and sometimes it is not so. You have read stories of those whose fear of flying and heights could be directly linked to their past life traumas, such as the Indian man trapped in rubble during an earthquake in the 1600s and the soldier on the battlements caught by a stray arrow and falling to his death in the 1500s. We have seen how starving to death or being sexually abused in a past life can have a direct impact on behaviour in this lifetime.

But it is not always that easy. Just because someone died from, say, pox or fever in a past life, does not mean they are doomed to the same fate this time round. The trauma can, however, leave a trace and show itself in ways that can be disruptive in this current lifetime.

Susie was just forty when she came to see me. She was in the aftermath of a nervous breakdown and was suffering from severe anxiety, mentioning her IBS almost as an afterthought. Susie understood enough about the way things work to know that taking all the tablets prescribed by her well-meaning doctor was not a route she wanted to follow in the longer-term, and she was looking for possible alternatives.

"Why don't we get right back there to the real underlying root cause?" I suggested.

She went into the deep state of relaxation very easily and we soon met Tabitha, who told me she was eight years-old, barefoot and dirty. She was outside in the countryside with fields and trees around her. She knew it was summer, she said, because of the trees and because it smelled warm. Tabitha was a very pleasant, chatty young lady, who explained that she was close to where she lived, in "a place made of stones." There were other similar stone places nearby.

I asked Tabitha about her family. Her mother was cooking, and she had a little brother called John who was six years-old. She thought she had a father but didn't know where he was. I asked what her mother was cooking and she replied, "Rabbit stew." I commented that that sounded rather nice and she corrected me. "It's always rabbit stew. It's not good. We're poor, so it's always rabbit stew."

Having set the scene, I next met Tabitha aged thirty-seven. She was very happy because she was married to Jock, had just had her first child and all was well. She told me that Jock was tall, he was wearing a shirt, brown trousers and shoes. They lived in a stone house close to where she lived when she was growing up. She had been with Jock a long time but this was their first child and they were both very happy. Tabitha told me she was in Scotland and she set the year as 1351, but didn't know if there was a king or a queen on the throne or who the local lord of the manor was.

Jock and Tabitha clearly led a simple life, as Jock hunted animals and birds from the woods nearby while Tabitha kept house,

"Sweeping, lots of sweeping." But the joy of having their first-born child, whom they called Peter, was shattered just a few days later when the baby died.

"I don't know what happened," Tabitha said. "He just died." She and Jock were devastated at the loss. I asked what would be done with Peter's body. "We're burying Peter with the other dead people," she told me. "There's a special place for dead people… the body is wrapped, it's put into the ground… me and Jock are holding hands, it's just us now."

Moving on through her life, I met Tabitha when she was fifty, the same age as Jock. Jock was now poorly, she told me, he had scarlet fever and she thought he was dying. He did indeed die just a few days later and was buried in the same 'special place for dead people' as baby Peter.

"Lots of people are dying," sighed Tabitha, although she confirmed that she herself was healthy at that time. However, she told me that she died later that year. She was in her bed in the stone house and she had scarlet fever, as Jock and so many others had. The doctor was with her. "He is wearing a mask," commented Tabitha, "and he is shaking his head, there's nothing he can do." I asked Tabitha what she could smell as she lay in her bed. "Death," she replied, "I smell death all around me…"

At the very end of her life, Tabitha looked back and noted times of sadness, of happiness and of regret. She was looking forward to being reunited with Jock when she passed.

In this lifetime, Susie had suffered multiple issues around her abdomen, which may well have been a residue from Tabitha losing baby Peter after just a few days. Whilst the enormous stress that Susie was under was no doubt a major factor in her IBS, the guilt that Tabitha felt when she survived scarlet fever when so many around her were dying could also have resonated with the guilt Susie felt about her own family and not being able to help more with their health problems.

However tenuous the links, however far-fetched they may seem, for me it is the healing that matters, and the feedback from Susie was that she felt much calmer, much more centred and her anxiety levels had dropped.

When Cathy came to see me she was just about thirty, married with a two month-old baby. She had suffered from anxiety since an early age and had been officially diagnosed with anxiety and OCD. This obsessive behaviour meant that her home was always spotlessly clean but included a number of 'rituals' or 'routines' that took time and energy. Cathy could see that new rituals were already creeping in concerning the new baby and she wanted to nip those, and the others, in the bud.

"I want to enjoy my baby," she said, "and for my baby to enjoy me."

Cathy was a spiritual lady and was used to relaxation and meditation techniques, so she went into the deep state of relaxation very easily. When we meet someone in a past life, my question about what they are wearing on their feet is a way of grounding them and a starting point to building a picture of who I am talking to. In this case the character was wearing black shoes and a long black dress which was, apparently, cheap (much to the disdain of the character, if the face that Cathy pulled was anything to go by).

The young lady introduced herself as Joanie and told me she was fifteen years-old. She was outside on the grass, having a picnic of jam sandwiches with her father and her little brother Dylan, three years-old. It was a sunny day and she could smell flowers. Joanie's mother was at home, not far away. Home was a big house with black beams. Joanie could not tell me the name of the village but the nearest big city was Manchester. She explained that her father had taken the children out for a picnic to get them away from the house as her mother was in bed.

"She's dying but we're not allowed to know."

Joanie told me there was a king on the throne but she didn't know his name. I asked her what year it was and she didn't know that either, so I suggested she should ask her father, which she did. It was 1846. Her father worked in a bank.

"He's strict. He wears a top hat and a suit." It seems her father was wearing a suit for the picnic with his children. I asked Joanie how she was feeling at the picnic. "I'm feeling sad," she said, "because I think my Mum's dying. I think it's going to be soon." I asked whether Joanie went to school and she said she did, but that she couldn't be bothered to listen.

When Joanie was twenty she was about to get married to a man called Peter, who worked with her father in the bank. Did she love Peter? "Nah." Did he love Joanie? "Yeah, I think so." She was marrying Peter because it's what her father wanted. "It's just something you have to do," her father had told her. Joanie confirmed that her mother had died of cancer.

Joanie and Peter got married in the village church of St George's. There were not many people there and Peter was an only child. Joanie described her wedding dress as white and lacy with long sleeves, quite fitted. The veil went right to the floor and had pearls in it. She told me she had auburn hair and that she was carrying lilies. There were no bridesmaids and her little brother was not a page boy. After the wedding, Joanie and Peter would be living in Peter's home, a small cottage with a thatched roof in the same village. After the wedding, the few guests went back to Joanie's father's cottage but the reception was "Nothing fancy" and there was no honeymoon. "Peter went back to work."

Three years later, Joanie was in hospital, having given birth to her first child, a daughter. Mother and baby were both well. Peter was there with her.

"He's boring," Joanie said. "He's so boring. He doesn't talk about anything, he's so miserable. He's as happy as he'll ever be about being a father. My father is happy and my little brother is happy too." It was clear that Joanie herself was not happy in her marriage. "I can't do anything about it. He's so miserable." She was living in Peter's small cottage, which she liked, and a room had been made ready for the new baby.

I asked Joanie how things were out in the wider world.

"Everyone's poor, no-one has any food, life is generally hard. My father's in the bank but no-one has any money, there's a recession. Things are going to get worse."

About a decade later, Joanie was thirty-two and not in a good place, saying, "I don't like being around anymore." She explained that her daughter Scarlett was fine, she was nine years-old, but that a son who was born just a few weeks ago had died after just two hours before they had named him. The baby had been buried at the village church. Joanie said the baby was in Heaven being looked after by angels. I offered my condolences on the loss of her baby and asked about Peter.

"He's miserable, he's not supportive, he just works all the time."

Visibly upset, Joanie said, "I want to be with my baby. I'm going to be with my baby. I'm going to end my life, I don't know how yet... Peter doesn't know or care about how I'm feeling, he only cares about Scarlett. He's still at the bank and he's still miserable.

"Scarlett's fine, though, she needs her father. She has brown wavy hair and green eyes and really red lips She's quite thin, very pretty. She goes to the local school and is a good pupil, she learns."

I moved Joanie forward to the end of her life.

"I killed myself, I took an overdose of drugs, anti-depressants. I was thirty-two. I did it in the bathroom. It was very peaceful, there was nobody else there." Just before she took that final out-breath, I asked Joanie to review her life. "It was miserable, boring, worthless," she said, her passing thought being, "Thank God it's over."

When I talked with the soul once the physical body of Joanie had died, I asked for a review of that lifetime.

"Never do anything that makes you unhappy," it said. "Be free."

HEALTH OF BODY AND MIND

When Cathy came back to the here and now, she had clearly been very moved by the past life experience and by the message of the soul. I commented that it was unusual that the girl's name in the past life was Joanie rather than Joan. "Oh, my goodness," she exclaimed. "Joanie is my grandmother's name. She's passed now but today is her birthday!"

There's no such thing as coincidence, really, is there?

It was about six weeks before I saw Cathy again. The difference was obvious as soon as she came through the door and she could not wait to tell me her news.

"We've moved house," she said, "and there were so many dramas, as there always are, but I didn't get upset once." I commented that she looked much brighter than the last time I had seen her, more confident and outgoing. She gave me some examples of the ways in which, before our work, her OCD would have been a major issue; but during, and since, the house move these issues had been brushed off and hadn't caused any problems at all.

"OCD?" she said. "What OCD? All gone!"

Rosemary, a lady in her seventies and a retired psychotherapist, came to see me to have her first ever past life regression session. She had experienced many other therapies and healing modalities in her life, she told me, and had come along to a talk I gave at a local village hall some months earlier. There were no pressing health or emotional issues as far as she was aware, but she was curious to know what would come up.

We met Jack who told me he was not sure how old he was, maybe around fifteen or so. Jack said he was barefoot and was wearing ragged trousers and a jerkin. I asked him where he was and he scrambled up a hill to get a better view for me. He said that behind him was a large building, a mental hospital that he was running away from.

"I'm not mental, I'm just a beggar," he said. "I don't live

anywhere in particular, I just survive and I'm happy. I've no wish to go back there."

Jack said he had no idea how long he had been in the large building, probably a year, and that it was not a nice place to be. He had no memory of having a family and seemed to have spent his life surviving from hand to mouth. He told me he was just picked up off the street and put into the mental hospital, he had no idea why. Jack was very upset because he'd had a dog when he was on the streets and he had no idea where the dog was now. As Rosemary started to move on the couch, so Jack became agitated.

"I need to get going, I can't hang around here, I need to move on."

Move on we did, and when I next met Jack he was in a city, so I asked him to describe what he saw around him.

"The buildings are of brick," he replied, with an impatient tone in his voice, "but that's not important. What's important is that I've just seen my dog. Someone has him on a lead. I'm going to follow them, to see where they go… I whistle to the dog and he turns, he knows me, he tries to come to me, he's desperate to get to me. The one who has him on a lead is dragging him away, getting angry… I have to be careful not to draw attention to myself, I don't want to go back to that place, never again…"

Jack followed the man to what he described as "a posh-looking house" with steps up to the front door. His dog was straining at the lead, trying to get to Jack, and the man was angrily dragging the dog up the steps and into the house. Jack explored the neighbourhood and found the back of the house. He had noted that the house was number twenty-three and the back gate had the same number. For a street urchin like Jack, a back gate was no barrier. He was up and over in no time and hiding behind a bush to wait until nightfall when, he hoped, the dog – a smooth-haired Jack Russell called Scruff – would be let out.

"I wait until night-time. It's getting dark now, I'm just waiting, waiting. There are steps down from the first floor of the house into the garden and below that is the kitchen… They let the dog out into the garden last thing at night. I whistle and he streaks down the garden. We're long gone! It's so lovely to have the little dog back again. I don't need him on a lead, we're off down the alley, making for the outskirts of the city and we're off. We were together for about three years before I was caught and he's the best friend I've ever had."

But when I next met Jack, he was desolate.

"Scruff got killed," he said. "We were in a small town by the sea at an inn. I'd been working there doing odd jobs for a bit, it was a wayside inn where coaches stopped. Scruff was chasing a cat or something and ran into the road, under a coach and horses. I think he got kicked by a horse and then run over by the wheels… I'm just looking at Scruff in the gutter, bloody and broken. I can't leave him there. I go over and pick him up. I take off my jacket and cradle him in it. There are lots of people around, it's only a dog to them and it's all my fault for causing trouble…

"I can't see the point without Scruff. I found my heart again with that dog, a new life. Escaping that mental hell, finding Scruff… and then seeing him killed like that… I'll take him with me. I'm not going to bury him, without Scruff there's nothing to live for…"

Jack took Scruff's body in his jacket and walked to the nearest beach, which was not far from the inn he had worked at. I asked Jack to look back over his life.

"It was a search for love, always. I found it in Scruff, that animal gave me sheer devotion. I never had that from a person." As he walked into the sea, and kept walking, with his beloved dog in his arms, Jack's passing thought was, "I don't ever want to be separated from my beloved companion. We shared life, hardship, fun. He was everything. Without him there was nothing. It was a real communion of souls."

The soul's review of that lifetime might surprise some people.

"It was a beautiful life in its way, a life outside of the status quo, outside of civilisation. It was a life lived to the full. Inevitably, there was conflict with civilisation." And the lesson from that lifetime? "The human species has lost contact with life, with what's meaningful – the joy of being under the stars, of having a companion to share it with. Scruff was part of my soul group, we have had many lives in one form or another together."

I was puzzled. One objective of the regression was to find a lifetime that related to Rosemary's issues around addiction.

"In that lifetime," the soul explained, "I was addicted to Scruff. Some people would say that I stole him from the man but that didn't mean anything to me, he was my dog. But he was more than that, he was like my other self, my twin. When I was looking after Scruff, cuddling him or feeding him, it was like looking after myself. He shared my experiences. Touching base with Scruff was like touching base with myself."

When the soul was preparing for this current lifetime, writing its script, I asked what the goals had been. The soul said it would like to help people find the companionship Jack had found with Scruff and acknowledged that it would be an enormous challenge to do that.

In her professional life, Rosemary had seen the results of her clients being distracted by and obsessed with material possessions and unrealistic expectations around money, careers, sex and status. She had striven to emphasise the need for healthy relationships and the value of companionship. The soul had also advised Rosemary to rediscover her sense of playfulness and fun, the freedom that Jack and Scruff shared and which in this lifetime had been curtailed by her role as full-time carer for a demanding partner.

Rosemary understood that lifetime and exactly how it resonated with her current life, a partner who needed a lot of care and attention but also kept her grounded – her Scruff in this life. Experiencing life as Jack, connecting with the soul in that way and having so much healing around the trauma, helped her to gain new insights and perspectives on her life and why it was unfolding as it was.

CHAPTER 10

Lives Cut Short or Wasted

If we accept the concept that a soul writes its own script for its next incarnation while it is in that so-called Bardo state, the life between lives, then we may think twice before making judgments about people who cross our path in this lifetime. We don't know what was on their list of goals or challenges, we don't know what that soul came here to achieve or to teach. We don't know, at least initially, what their purpose might be in our own lifetime.

It may be, for instance, that there is just one thing for them to 'complete' in this lifetime and so the lifespan is short. Perhaps there is a lesson, say, to teach compassion, and so the soul may be born with or develop physical, mental or serious health issues that will challenge their immediate family and help them to complete their tasks in this lifetime.

I do understand that this statement may not go down well with some people. There are inevitable questions.

"Why would someone choose to be born so badly disabled that they are confined to a wheelchair?"

"Why would a child choose to die so young when they have their whole life ahead of them?"

My answer is, simply, that we have no way of knowing what that soul's journey is and it is not for us to judge that. Consider Professor Stephen Hawking, for example, one of the most brilliant scientific minds of our times. When he was in his late teens, he contracted Amyotrophic Lateral Sclerosis (ALS, otherwise known as Lou Gehrig's disease), an incurable degenerative neuromuscular disease that killed Lou Gehrig when he was thirty-seven. Science and medicine have both improved enormously since those early days and, with determination, a strong will to live and vastly improved technology, Hawking lived to be seventy-six.

In that time, his contribution to modern Science was enormous. His theory of exploding black holes drew upon both Relativity theory and quantum mechanics, and he also worked with space-time singularities. Did he really choose to put so many severe obstacles in his own path? Was he perhaps balancing some karma from a previous life? We can never know. And the point is that it is not for us to judge or to pity.

Just because a life is short or disabled does not mean that it is not in line with the soul's plan. And it does not mean that there are not lessons to be learned or great achievements to be made.

Barry was in his mid-seventies when he came to see me. I already knew him and was aware that he had been on his spiritual pathway for a very long time. He had studied many ideas and healing modalities and was interested to see what a past life session would add to his understanding of why he was here this time round. When I asked if there were any particular issues in this life that he felt might come up, he mentioned always being hungry as a child, crying a lot and, as he put it, "Lots to do with mother."

He slid into a deep state of relaxation like an old pro and easily found the door he wanted to go through into a past life. We met a young boy who introduced himself as Bob and said he was around four or five years-old. He told me he was dressed in short trousers, a shirt and slippers. He was indoors in what felt like a dining room since he could see a big table and that the place felt familiar – it could be his home.

Barry felt "something like cobwebs" over his face and wanted to brush them away. I allowed him to do that, while remaining in a deep state of relaxation, and when we returned to the life of Bob the scene had changed.

"It's dark, it feels like a cave. I can see, I'm just inside a cave and I can feel the rocks around me. It's dark behind me and I feel trapped here. Is the tide coming in?" I asked Bob what he was doing in the cave. "I don't know, really, I just went in to have a look around, I was exploring. I just wanted to go into the cave and look but I got stuck. I'm alone here and it's like I'm trapped somehow. The cave is at the coast." I asked what was preventing him from getting out of the cave. "I don't know, I feel as though I'm lost. I can see an opening, I can sense the way out but I can't move…" I encouraged Bob to try to move towards the opening. "I'm trying to take small steps but I don't seem to be moving… my left leg aches, it feels very cold…"

I felt it was relevant to find out what happened before Bob got to the cave so, instead of moving him forward, I moved him back so that he could fill in the story.

"I'm five years-old. I'm on the beach. I can see this cave up there and I decide to climb up and have a look." Where were his family? "I'm here on the beach on my own, I'm exploring," he said. "The rest of the family are not here. They don't know where I am, they're doing what they want to do and I'm doing what I want to do.

"I climbed up to the cave and went inside but as I went further inside it got dark and I didn't like it, so I turned to come back out again. But I've fallen down and hurt my leg. I fell over some rocks, I lost my footing. My leg's at a funny angle. It's cold and I can't move it, it hurts too much. The tide's coming in and I'm too high. I'm frightened there's something behind me in the cave. I don't think there is, but I'm still frightened."

I let Bob sit with the situation and let the story unfold, without pushing him forward too much.

"The tide's coming in… I'll be cut off but I'll be safe. My family doesn't know where I am, I just said I was off out exploring, you know… It's night-time now, I can see the moon. I can't move my leg. I feel frightened and I'm getting hungry… I think they're looking for me but they won't see me up here, they can't see me… I can't get to the entrance of the cave. I feel so lonely. It's dark out there, they're not going to find me… I don't even know if they are looking for me…"

Next morning, Bob was still there in the cave.

"It's getting light, the tide's out. It's quiet and I can see a little bit of the beach from here but I can't see any people." I ask Bob if he can tell me where he is. "We're on holiday. I can see a small pier further up the coast… I think it's Felixstowe. We're staying in lodgings but I don't know the name of the place… It's light again now but they're not going to find me. I'm going to sleep, I'm so tired…"

The end of his life was not far away. Bob told me he was just going to go to sleep and that would be that. I asked him to look back over his short life and he said simply, "I was lonely and hungry. I was always hungry." His passing thought was, "They're not going to find me."

The soul confirmed what Bob had told me before he died. "It was a lonely life. He had no friends, he had to explore on his own, to make his own world. He never had anyone to play with."

Barry then spontaneously went into another past life!

Here we found Thomas, a young boy who said he was five years-old, he was barefoot and wearing rags. He was indoors in a house that he felt he knew but he couldn't see it clearly, he didn't know why. He explained that he worked at the house as a skivvy lad in the scullery, where he had been for as long as he could remember. There was nobody else around to tell him what to do but he knew he had chores to do. Thomas told me he could just see out of a window and that it was very dreary outside. I asked him how he was feeling.

"I feel abandoned. I'm all on my own, I'm lonely, I'm frightened… There's no food, there's nothing to eat, there's no water…" The end of that short life was near. "I'm sitting down on the floor. I'm still five… I'm so weak, there's no food, no water… I've been abandoned, left all on my own. I can't get out, I've tried, the door won't open. I can't hear anything, there's no noise at all… I shouted and shouted but there was nothing, nothing. I'm sliding onto the floor now, I'm so tired, I've got no more energy, I'm just so weary."

Thomas' passing thought was, "Why have I been abandoned?" The soul's review was, "It was short and it was sad. He felt so alone and so abandoned for his whole life."

When the soul was preparing for this current lifetime, I asked what the goals were. "To find my true self, my spiritual self, and to understand my place in the universe." The challenges were going to be great, to relive his traumas, to overcome adversity, to find love, compassion and understanding. He would need to persevere, be tenacious and go with love.

There was considerable healing to be done around both of those short and not-so-sweet lives, after which Barry reported feeling much lighter and much freer. He said that he had felt the rays of unconditional love from the 'higher realm' as the soul was connecting, which was overwhelming.

The parallels between the two lives are obvious and resonated totally with Barry's issues in this lifetime of always being hungry, always feeling alone, and having a sense of being abandoned or not being found.

We can only imagine how Bob's sense of adventure turned to fear and foreboding, and then the understanding that he was going to die there alone and hungry in the cave. Even on holiday, it seemed, he was left to make his own entertainment; there did not seem to be too much concern about where he was going or what he would be doing. Nowadays, it's hard to imagine leaving a five year-old to roam a beach and climb the rocks without keeping an eye on them, isn't it? And as for poor little Thomas, all on his own in the scullery – whoever abandoned him there and why? How long had he been there? Did nobody miss him? Like Bob, when the end of his life finally came, he was just too weary to do anything except slide to the floor and sleep, still beset by those questions of who and why...

Even though the lives were short, they were exactly what we needed to find to resolve the issues of this life for Barry, and to set the soul free from carrying that burden any longer.

Dan came to see me because, by his own admission, his life was a mess even though he was only in his mid-twenties. He felt he was going nowhere fast and needed some sort of direction. We had managed to clear one major issue in previous sessions and he was curious to see what a past life journey would reveal.

Through the door to his chosen past life we met James, a man in his fifties. It was a modern past life, James was wearing sandals, shorts and a tee-shirt, and he was alone on a beach somewhere although he could not tell me where. It was a very bright, sunny day, and he could see rocky cliffs to his left and a long stretch of white sand beach around him. The sea, he said, was cold. I asked James what year it was and he said, "Sixty-four." I asked if there was a king or a queen on the throne but he couldn't tell me. What was he doing there on the beach? "I don't think it's my choice to be here. I would prefer to be home but I have no idea about where or what home is…"

Some twenty years later, James was sitting in an armchair in front of an open fire. He was seventy years-old, he was at home and he was alone. I asked him to tell me about his life.

"I'm old, the house is old and it's dark and dingy." I encouraged James to go and look in a mirror and tell me what he saw. "I have a rugged face," he replied, "brown eyes, grey hair – it was brown once – and I am tall and skinny. I was strong once but not now. I have no disabilities."

And yet, there in his armchair in front of the fire, James passed away. He just didn't want to be here anymore. Before he died, I asked him to look back over his life. He sighed.

"It was a lonely life. I never married and I have no money. It was a waste." His passing thought was, "I wish I'd done more and had more."

"It was indeed a wasted life," the soul agreed. "He did very little with it." Despite that, the soul was eager to come into this current lifetime when the time came – "I want to make more of it this time" – and the advice was, "Stay strong, remember your purpose."

Finding that life was a shock to Dan. He had found someone twice his age who had done nothing with his life, had no story to tell, and died alone and penniless regretting what might have been. And that someone had been him! It acted as a real wake-up call for him and, with all of the healing work that we did around that lifetime, allowed him to have a much more clear, positive perspective about his future.

Sophie, a complementary therapist in her late forties, came to me to find out more about past life regression. In her bodywork therapy, her clients sometimes released 'stuck stuff' or had flashes to past lives, and Sophie was curious to experience for herself a full past life session.

We met Zana, a young man in his mid-twenties who was wearing open sandals and a plain beige, knee-length robe. Zana was outdoors under a clear blue sky and blazing sun with sand all around him. He explained that he was a servant, he worked for the master, a very rich man who lived in a big palace on a hill not far away. The palace was made of solid stone and was very strong. It was Zana's job to run errands for the master and today he had been sent down the hill to find a particular person and give them a message. Zana was arriving at a small market looking for the man and I asked him what he could see around him there.

"There are people selling all kinds of wares," he said, "gold-looking jugs, tableware and platters, and there are goats and chickens." He said it smelled hot, dry and dusty. The man that Zana was looking for was a stallholder here. "The master is doing deals with this man." The name of the man was given as something like Bal-al, and he was wearing a long tunic with trousers underneath. Zana said he was quite fat and his hair was thin and wispy. I asked Zana for the name of the nearest town or city and he said it was Kapoor, which was two days away by camel.

"The master buys and sells treasures, gold, pretty things," he told me. "He knows lots of people. They are not all good people." I asked him to tell me more about the master and he said, "Sometimes I'm beaten, the master has a temper, he's an impatient man." What about Zana's family? He had a mother, who was very old, but he was not married and had no children. He lived with the other servants in a separate part of the palace to the master. "I'm tired of it, it's always the same. I'd like to be free to go away from the master, to be free and find things I can do… I'd like some goats, to have my own home, to care for myself, not to be ruled… I can't see that happening. It's very hard here, I have to survive."

When I next met Zana, some ten years later, he was much more positive.

"I've got lots of goats, lots of them! I got lucky, someone was kind to me and I got lucky. I was on an errand for the master, talking to a man who didn't really like the master and he asked if I wanted to move away. He said he could make it possible, I'd be helping him but not like the master, he would give me some goats and a small home… I take care of his land and I'm allowed to keep my goats on his land. I have to see off people who are trying to steal this man's herds and I tell the man who they are… This man has lots of land and lots of herds."

Zana gave this man's name as something like Jaffar and said that he was now some distance from the master, in a village called what sounded like Milium. He said that he had been with Jaffar for eight years and that he was better than the master, he was not mean. He still didn't have a family but he had friends, the younger men who helped to work and look after the land and the herds.

"They are younger than me but we all spend time together eating and drinking and talking and laughing." Zana told me he was happy, he felt safe and he felt lucky. "It doesn't worry me that there's no woman in my life, not now. The others laugh at me and tease me, they try to get me interested in some of the women in the village. Some of the women are just horrible. I can't be bothered. I'm quite happy on my own, I feel safer on my own. I don't answer to anyone and I am my own master."

By the time Zana was forty-eight, Jaffar had died and his son had taken over the lands so Zana now worked for him.

"I'm in a market with a small tent. There's lots of noise and bustle and deals being done. I can hear voices and animals crying and I can smell food. Meat is being cooked somewhere close by." Zana was there to do a trade, to sell some of his herd of goats. "I need some money and I don't need so many goats now I'm getting older. I just want a nicer place to rest in so I can have a young boy look after the herd for me… I'm old, I'm tired, I've had a hard life. My chest is bad, I've had enough."

Zana reached the end of his life just a year later.

"I'm at home on the floor, curled up. The young boy who looks after my herd is here with me… I'm just worn out, my chest is not right, I can't breathe properly. The doctor is a long way away and it would be too late by the time he got here."

I asked Zana to look back over his life.

"It was a hard life, hard work, and it's been lonely. I regret that I didn't find a wife in the market. My friends were right. I learned that we need to share ourselves." His passing thought was, "I want to be my own master."

"It was too single, too alone, too sad," the soul observed sympathetically. "He learned not to be under a master and he became a master, but he was not a good master to himself."

The goals for this current lifetime were to learn enlightenment, to share the light and the love, to reach out to others, to serve others and help them find the light. Yet the challenges would be considerable.

"I need to learn and feel the darkness through pain and sorrow. There will be lots of emotional suffering and people will push me to the limit. I will need to be strong, dig deep in time of trouble to discover my inner spark by finding joy and by finding the freedom to be myself."

The theme of Zana wanting to be his own master clearly struck a chord with Sophie, as did the longing for freedom from commitments. There was a wry smile as she acknowledged, as Zana had done, that such a route could lead to loneliness and regrets in later life. She was surprised by the intensity of the experience.

"I really could smell that burning meat in the market," she said, "and the emotions at the end were strong too."

That is one of the lovely things about past life work – the senses don't lie and the emotions don't lie. It is not at all uncommon for the client on the couch to move or cry at a particular moment in the story, or to wrinkle their nose in disgust at a smell wafting around their nostrils. Sophie came in thinking that her past life session would be an easy ride, a bit of interesting fun. Instead, her unconscious, her higher self, took her to just the right lifetime to be reminded of exactly what she needed to know at this time.

CHAPTER 11

Modern Research

As the pioneers of past life regression therapy paved the way, so others followed in their footsteps and nowadays there are many, many therapists working in this field. Enormous gratitude is due to those who have written books, produced videos and set up training courses to spread the word and, in the process, establish protocols and standards for this work. In this chapter we meet some of the modern researchers. You will see that they all have their own approach to what is a very broad topic, yet the underlying principles are the same: many issues that are holding people back in this lifetime can be traced to trauma in a past lifetime. And once that trauma is healed in the past, the client finds that healing takes place in this lifetime too.

Therapists are researchers too, in their own way. They may not investigate cases and conduct field studies as, say, Ian Stevenson, Jim Tucker or Roy Stemman. Yet they work directly with clients, recording their case studies and analysing the results, honing their methodology and pushing the boundaries of what is possible by accessing the unconscious mind.

Dr Morris Netherton (1935 – 2020) was a qualified psychologist and one of the first in this field. Indeed, his book *Past Lives Therapy* was the first to be published on the subject.[9] Over a period of forty-five years, Netherton worked with some forty thousand clients and developed his own way of addressing the conscious and unconscious parts of a client's brain.

In his second book, *Strangers in the Land of Confusion*, he expounded his theory that the same patterning that causes, for instance, anxiety or fear or trauma in an individual also exists in families, towns, countries and even widely across the world.[10]

'The same confusion that will destroy a woman's immune system and allow cancer to take over will also compromise the immune system of an entire sub-culture and allow the development of AIDS. One man's self-destructive thoughts which stem from low self-esteem are also found in starving refugees who are forced to believe they are ethnically inferior and deserve to be punished and killed. The unfounded fears of an individual who suffers from mysterious panic attacks are the same fears that create public policy, which spends vast sums of money for national defence while ignoring the needs of education and public health services. The patterns of fear and confusion found in individual consciousness are the same patterns found in group consciousness.'

As you may imagine, that was controversial even then! Personally, I would not go as far as he does in relating personal issues to the world as a whole, but he does have a very valid point. As the saying goes, 'Thoughts are things, and things have wings.'

In other words, it is not only our *actions* that have an impact on others; our words and even our *thoughts* have energy and therefore ripple out into the collective sea of energy waves we all live in. You could think of it as a cauldron of soup from which we all feed. It starts

---

[9] Published by Morrow (1978)
[10] CreateSpace Independent Publishing Platform (2015)

off being neutral, without flavouring, but then people's thoughts, words and actions add to the soup, be they negative or positive. Those who live in a state of stress, fear and anxiety, will add those flavours to the soup, whilst those who live in a state of calm, happiness and optimism, will add those different flavours.

We all take in all of those ingredients, whether we want to or not. So if individuals are focused on fear and worry, as so many have been during recent world crises, for instance, that is the energy going into the collective soup and influencing the wider community, the human collective. Equally, this is why spiritual 'light workers' have been stepping up their efforts to add more positivity and optimism into the soup, to restore some balance.

Dr Brian Weiss (b.1944) is probably better known than Netherton to those outside the immediate arena of past life work. He is a psychiatrist, hypnotherapist and prolific author of bestselling books on aspects of past life regression. Dr Weiss, like several others in the fields of psychology and psychiatry, stumbled across the power of past life regression virtually by accident when he was working with a client whom he called Catherine.

The story is told in his book *Many Lives, Many Masters*.[11] Catherine suffered from recurring nightmares, panic attacks and chronic anxiety, which had been getting worse. Dr Weiss had been working with her for some eighteen months with no tangible results. He then tried hypnosis, which did unlock some of Catherine's traumas in this lifetime but nevertheless the nightmares and anxiety continued. In the next session, Dr Weiss decided to regress her to earlier in her childhood; they got to the age of two, but Catherine could not recall anything of significance. And then he instructed Catherine, "Go back to the time from which your symptoms arise."

And, just like that, Catherine became Aronda, in 1863 BCE. Dr Weiss had inadvertently used a variation on those magic words,

---

[11] Published in paperback by Piatkus (1994)

"Go back to the first time when…" He had given the client's unconscious permission to access whatever and whenever it needed in order to find the root cause of the issue. That in itself was as surprising to Dr Weiss as it was to Catherine, but the positive results spoke for themselves.

There were more surprises to come, for Catherine found that she was a natural 'channel'. In other words, she could apparently connect with beings from other worlds and they could speak through her. If Dr Weiss was sceptical about the whole process of past life regression, which he was, then this was definitely uncharted territory for an orthodox psychiatrist. Yet the 'messages' that came through contained highly personal details about his own life and family that Catherine could not possibly have known, so he was forced to think again about reality, consciousness and the secrets of life and death.

Dr Weiss continues to be a wonderful advocate for the use of past life regression for healing. Apart from his many books, there are a lot of video interviews with him available online in which he speaks eloquently about the subject. Here are quotes from some of these:

"The soul is the enduring part of us that doesn't die at the death of the physical body, it is immortal, eternal. It's our real nature."

"As people come to think of themselves more as spiritual beings and understand the nature of the soul, the deeper nature of the mind, values start to change. We shouldn't attach to material things. The soul doesn't need any of that, it just understands about love in all its different manifestations."

"The concept of reincarnation is that you have more than one chance to get it correct, evolving along this spiritual pathway. It's really learning about love, compassion and kindness."

Dr Roger Woolger (1944 – 2011) was born in England but later settled in America. He was a Jungian analyst, regression therapist and author of several books on regression and healing. He held degrees in Psychology and Philosophy from Oxford University, in

Comparative Religion from Kings College London, and studied at the Jung Institute in Switzerland.

His life and career path seemed set and straightforward until he agreed to be a guinea pig for a friend of his who was researching regression techniques. Woolger found himself in the middle of a battle as a rough Cathar mercenary who met a bloody end. This added another dimension to his own research into past life healing, including past life memories, consciousness and archetypes.

He put forward three possible views on past life memories. The first, 'Positivist or Tabula Rasa', stated that the mind is a blank slate: we only have one life and one identity and therefore all psychological disturbances must result from this current lifetime. Reports of past lives therefore come from the unconscious imagination, from books, TV, films and so on, all muddled as though in a dream. This is what Théodore Flournoy first called Cryptomnesia in his 1899 book *From India To the Planet Mars*.[12]

The second view was 'Great Memory', whereby we can all tap into a layer of the unconscious mind that is universal, a massive collective memory bank. This has variously been called the Great Mind, the Akashic Records or the Collective Unconscious.

His third view quoted William Wordsworth:

'Our birth is but a sleep and a forgetting.
The soul that rises with us, our life's star,
hath had elsewhere its setting and cometh from afar.' [13]

In this view, Woolger suggested that the soul has lived many lives in numerous bodies, collecting merit or demerit points as a consequence of what it has done before.

He developed what he called the Deep Memory Process, a powerful technique that brings together principles of past life

---

[12] Reprinted by Princeton University Press (1994)
[13] Ode on Intimations of Immortality from Recollections of Early Childhood

regression and elements of Jungian philosophy. It does not use hypnosis but rather encourages the client to 'go back', to find the memory that they need to look at. This work continues today with training programmes and therapists around the world.

In his book *Other Lives, Other Selves*, he wrote, "It doesn't matter whether you believe in reincarnation or not. The unconscious mind will almost always produce a past life story when invited in the right way. Even if the conscious mind is highly sceptical, the unconscious is a true believer!"[14]

Dr Michael Newton (1931 – 2016) held a doctorate in Counselling Psychology and was a certified hypnotherapist in his native America. He worked as a psychologist in both private practice and as a corporate consultant. It was in the late 1960s that he worked with a client who complained of severe pains in his shoulder; conventional medicine could find no cause for the pain, suggesting that it was psychosomatic.

In a deep state of relaxation, the words "Go back to the time when…" took the client into the thick of the Battle of the Somme. Dr Newton asked many questions while the client was there in the trenches so that the story could be verified. After the session, the client professed himself healed and Dr Newton was able to confirm all of the information he had been given.

Work with another client led him not to a past life but to a 'life between lives', and this became the area that his pioneering research work focused on in his quest to answer three key questions: Who am I? What is my life purpose? Where am I going when I die?

In the book *Memories of the Afterlife*,[15] a collection of case studies produced by members of the Newton Institute, Dr Newton wrote, "As a result of the forces of reincarnation, we are all products of our past physical lives on Earth as well as our spiritual soul experiences

---

[14] Published by Dolphin Books (1987)
[15] Published by Llewellyn Publications, U.S. (2009)

between lives. The soul of every person on this planet retains all former Karmic influences of cause and effect from many sources and these forces impact our current feelings and behaviour."

Over the course of thirty years of research, Dr Newton worked with some seven thousand clients and his resulting *Life Between Lives (LBL) Technique*™ is said to map a working model of the spirit world.

"All of our research with thousands of cases," he said, "clearly shows the afterlife to be a realm of love, compassion, forgiveness and justice." The Newton Institute, which he established, continues his work into life between lives research and offers training courses on that technique for practitioners around the globe.

Dolores Cannon (1931 – 2014) introduced another aspect to regression work, including 'off-world connections'. Married at twenty, she spent the next two decades travelling and raising a family with her US Navy husband Johnny. Land-based by the 1960s, Dolores and Johnny were using simple hypnosis for habits such as smoking and weight control.

A lady was referred to them for relaxation as she suffered from high blood pressure and kidney stones. During the session, the client slipped into a life as a 1920s Chicago flapper, complete with change of vocal patterns and body mannerisms. Over the following months, they regressed this same woman through five distinct lifetimes, apparently to when she was created by God. This incredible story was the basis of Dolores' first book *Five Lives Remembered*.[16]

Largely because there were no set rules or protocols around past life regression at that time, Dolores and Johnny made up their own. After many years and thousands of clients, she came to understand that the information that came through in past life work came from the subconscious. Her *Quantum Healing Hypnosis Technique*® is

---

[16] Published by Ozark Mountain Publishing (2009)

based on using a mix of voice, imagery and visualisation to establish contact with the subconscious.

It was, however, her more metaphysical work that was to bring her into the public eye and make her name. From the mid-1980s her work took on another dimension, quite literally, when she became interested in the areas of UFO and ET (extra-terrestrial) investigations. While in England exploring crop circles, Cannon met a woman who claimed she had been having abduction experiences. One session with the woman had more than thirty observers and they all heard the woman describe interaction with ETs and multigenerational relationships between Earth families and ET races.

Cannon went on to write about 'the Three Waves of Volunteers', souls who agreed to come to planet Earth after the bombings of Hiroshima and Nagasaki in 1945 to help humanity with the journey towards its transition to higher frequencies. Her book *The Three Waves of Volunteers and the New Earth* tells that story.[17] Dolores Cannon died in 2014 but her daughter Julia has picked up the reins at the Quantum Healing Hypnosis Academy, which continues to offer training in this particular modality.

In a court of law, a case has to be proven beyond reasonable doubt, and so it should be with cases of past life regression. The master of past life research, Dr Ian Stevenson, was always very careful about terminology. In his book *European Cases of the Regression Type*, he opens by saying, "This book reports cases suggestive of reincarnation in Europe."[18] Note that he does not mention 'proof'; to do that, solid evidence would be needed.

One of the many challenges Stevenson faced when doing his research into children who seemed to remember past lives in India

---

[17] Published by Ozark Mountain Publishing (2011)
[18] Published by McFarland & Co (2009)

was the lack of written records. It was all word-of-mouth rather than hard-copy factual names, dates and information. Nowadays, though, people are regressing to past lives in times when there were accurate records and this makes it much easier to validate the information given.

One of the most widely reported cases in recent years was that of James Leiniger, who was born in 1998. His parents reported that from the age of around two he started to have nightmares, always with the same theme: he was in an aircraft that had been shot down, the plane was in flames and there was no way out. As James grew up, he began to draw images, always of the same type of aeroplane, in flames. He showed great interest in and knowledge of WWII aircraft even though he had not studied anything about them. He told his parents the type of aircraft he flew in and the name of the aircraft carrier that was its base, off the coast of Japan.

His parents, initially sceptical, began to wonder about a past life and started their own research. The US military authorities confirmed the details that James had provided, including the names of the other men in his squadron. From old photographs he identified himself as James Huston. Arrangements were made for the living James to meet the surviving members of the team and, when the young boy met the old men, he knew them all by name and nickname and asked after their families.

The authorities, surprised as they were, could not argue with this and agreed to take James and his parents out to sea, to the spot James had correctly identified as being where he was shot down. A simple ceremony was held to honour James Huston and bring closure. From that time on, the nightmares stopped, and young James started drawing images of dolphins instead.

It's a compelling story, isn't it, and at first glance has all of the elements of a convincing case. But researcher Michael Sudduth thought otherwise. He undertook a two-year investigation to debunk the story put together by the Leiniger parents in their book *Soul Survivor: The Reincarnation of a World War II Fighter Pilot*.[19]

Sudduth claims that the parents changed their story multiple times and suggests that they may even have given suggestions to young James in order to encourage a particular line of narrative. In January of 2022, Sudduth reported in his online blog that the Bigelow Institute for Consciousness Studies had recently awarded Bruce Leiniger, the father of young James, $20,000 for an essay in which he presented his son's story and claimed that it was 'definitive proof of reincarnation'. Sudduth then published a detailed critique of the essay, to debunk the story yet again.

So even with an apparent wealth of information to support a case – names, dates, photographs, locations and so on – it is still possible that things are not as they seem. We have no way of knowing whether the Leiniger version of the story is correct or if Sudduth was right to call them out. And that, of course, is a constant challenge with these situations.

The case of Jenny Cockell, however, seemingly cannot be disproved because she went back to her own past life and found her own children! The story is told in her book *Yesterday's Children*.[20] Jenny explains that, for as long as she could remember, she'd had dreams of a lady called Mary at the end of her life, desperately worried about the children she was leaving behind. She would often awake in tears at the strength of emotions those nightmares had stirred in her.

As an introverted child growing up in Northamptonshire, UK, Jenny was reluctant to share her nightmares even with her mother. She understood somehow that, in that dream state, it was not death itself that was so frightening but rather the sense of loss and grief

---

[19] Published by Hay House UK (2017)
[20] Published by Piatkus (1993)

at leaving the children. In those dreams, she remembered Mary's children individually and collectively, she could describe them physically and by their different characters and temperaments, all seven or eight of them, she thought. She could also remember a cottage in detail, and just knew all about aspects of daily life in the village. As these fragments came together, Jenny realised that the time period was around 1898 to the 1930s and that the place was Ireland.

While still young, Jenny sat with a map of Ireland to identify the place and consistently recognised Malahide, north of Dublin. She was careful to record all the details about Mary, knowing in herself that it was a past life, even if such talk would receive a very lukewarm reception in her family and beyond. By the time she was sixteen, Jenny had decided that finding Mary would be her mission; but there was still school, exams and daily life to cope with.

As she matured and then married, Jenny needed to focus more on the here and now, although sights or sounds or smells would still trigger very vivid memories of Mary's life. Jenny had her own first child in 1979 and her second in 1983; through them she was able to experience for herself, rather than vicariously through Mary, the maternal feelings of love, protection and guilt regarding her offspring.

It was with the blessing of her husband, her mother and close friends, that Jenny then set off on her quest to find Mary. She came across the work of Dr Ian Stevenson and that was hugely reassuring to her. At this time, she was exploring her awakening psychic abilities and this led to her meeting a man who practised hypnosis. In the very first session, she found Mary and such was the power of the experience that the hypnotist asked her to undertake more sessions to be recorded and documented.

In June 1989, Jenny finally managed to visit Malahide and put more pieces into the puzzle, including the surname of Sutton. Various strands of research were now under way and she discovered that the children had been put into an orphanage when Mary died. Continued research eventually uncovered all eight of Mary's children: Sonny, born 1919; Mary, born 1922; Jeffrey (also known as James), born 1924; Philomena, born 1925; Christopher, born 1926; Francis (Frank), born 1928; Bridget, born 1929; and Elizabeth, born 1932. One other baby had died and Mary herself died in 1933. Her daughter Mary had died aged twenty-four, before Jenny was born. However, eventually Jenny made contact with a daughter of Jeffrey, who confirmed there had indeed originally been eight children. She was also able to contact Jeffrey himself – her own son, now considerably older than her!

In September 1990, Jenny was able to visit Mary's oldest son Sonny in person. He was very open to meeting Jenny and, unsurprisingly, they had plenty to talk about. Further work managed to track down almost all of the children, who had spread far and wide, and two years later a family reunion was arranged when Sonny finally met some of his siblings:

What an extraordinary story! Just imagine finding your own children from a past life, who are now much older than you, and introducing yourself as their mother. Mary had died just twenty-one years before Jenny was born – that's quite a quick turnaround in reincarnation cases – and obviously the recent memories were still clear enough and strong enough to come through to Jenny, who was herself psychic and so more sensitive to mental energies.

Does this case qualify as 'beyond reasonable doubt'?

CHAPTER TWELVE

Gifts Carried Forward

Could it be that people who display extraordinary gifts in this life have brought them from a previous life? There are those who think this very likely. Why not? If trauma can be carried forward, then why shouldn't skills, gifts and talents be carried forward too? We have all heard of child prodigies who excel at a particular subject such as Mathematics or music.

What about baseball? One of the modern case studies that seems to pass the test of 'beyond all reasonable doubt' is that of Christian Haupt, born in the USA in 2009. It is thought that he may be the reincarnation of the famous baseball player Lou Gehrig, who died in 1941. His story has been told in the book *The Boy Who Knew Too Much*, written by his mother Cathy Byrd.[21]

By the age of two, Christian insisted on wearing nothing but baseball kit, both at home and at school. He had no interest in toys or

---

[21] Published by Hay House Inc (2017)

even in television; all he wanted to do was have his parents pitch balls at him. When he was two years-old, his mother took him see the LA Dodgers play in their home stadium, which he loved. Mother and son returned with a friend the next day for a tour of the stadium, and Cathy videoed him 'in action' on the dirt track at the edge of the field.

This became a one-minute video uploaded to YouTube along with a request that he should pitch the first ball at a Dodgers' game. The video was noticed by a casting agent for an Adam Sandler film who was looking for a young child good at baseball, and Christian got the part. While on the film set, which was set inside a baseball stadium, mother and son walked past a large photograph of famous player Babe Ruth. Christian stopped, looked at the picture and got quite upset.

"I don't like him," the boy said, "he was mean to me." Later that evening, as he was being put to bed, the boy told his mother, "I used to be a tall baseball player, I was tall like Daddy."

That started a journey of discovery, especially for Cathy who, as a devout churchgoer, had never entertained the concept of past lives. But as he began to talk more, so Christian revealed more details about his 'other life'.

"The Dodgers used to play in New York," he said. "We played games during the day because there were no lights on the field back then."

The reference to Babe Ruth had given Cathy a timeframe at least and she managed to find a photograph of the Yankees team, for whom Babe Ruth played, taken in 1927. She showed it to Christian who immediately pointed out "Dumb Babe Ruth". Cathy asked if there was anyone in the picture who didn't like Babe Ruth and the boy pointed to a player with dimples.

"That's me." Further research put the name Lou Gehrig to the player with dimples.

As Christian provided more information, Cathy's research confirmed all the details he gave to be absolutely true. Lou Gehrig and

Babe Ruth had been best friends for years but, following a major falling-out, did not speak or acknowledge each other for seven years until Gehrig's retirement speech in 1941, shortly before he died. He was only thirty-eight years-old. Cathy also showed Christian a photograph of Lou Gehrig's parents and asked what their names were, feeding him with all sorts of false names before slipping in the right ones. Her son got them both right. Cathy was even more profoundly surprised when the boy pointed to Lou Gehrig's mother.

"Mommy, you were her," he said, the implication being that not only had Lou Gehrig reincarnated as Christian, but his then mother had reincarnated as his current mother too!

In her research, Cathy came across the work done by Dr Ian Stevenson. As we have seen, he had conducted thousands of interviews with children who claimed to have remembered past lives, and with thousands more adults too. Stevenson's scientific, analytical methods had led him to the conclusion that the phenomenon of life before life was indeed genuine. This only made Christian's accounts all the more fascinating for his mother.

In the spring of 2012, Adam Sandler's film *That's My Boy* was released, featuring Christian as the young baseball player. This created a fresh wave of publicity and, just after his fourth birthday, the boy got his wish and took the first pitch at a Dodgers' game. Observers noted that Christian had the same stance as Lou Gehrig when he was about to pitch a ball, with the same warm-up routine and gestures. Some had also commented to Cathy, having seen the film or seen Christian play, that the way he slid into bases having hit the ball was just the same as Lou Gehrig had done, with one arm up and one dragging.

Cathy eventually turned to therapist and past life researcher Dr Jim Tucker, who met the family and spoke at length with them. Dr Tucker had come across similar cases and was able to reassure Cathy that by the time he was six or seven years-old, the memories of his life as Lou Gehrig would probably start to fade.

Cathy herself, though, was now becoming more intrigued by the idea that she might have been Lou Gehrig's mother in that past life, and she found a past life therapist recommended by a long-time friend. Even in the first session it became clear that, yes, it seemed to be true. Names, dates, places and other details were revealed – well beyond what she had found in her researches for Christian – and, with them, a whole range of emotions and 'knowings'. When she returned from that first regression session and told Christian that not only did she believe that he had been Lou Gehrig but that she had also been his mother, it was a very special moment indeed for both of them.

As Dr Jim Tucker had predicted, the memories of the life of Lou Gehrig started to fade by the time Christian reached six years-old, but this did not affect his extraordinary talent for baseball, which he continues to enjoy to this day.

Miranda was just thirty when she came to see me. She worked with horses, training and teaching, and was seeking answers to some questions around her work as well as hoping to overcome a fear of jumps that had been triggered when she'd had a nasty fall. This was not her first session with me and she was comfortable with the routine of allowing herself to sink into a deep state of relaxation.

In the past life we met Emily, who told me she was twenty-three years-old, barefoot and wearing ragged clothes. She was on a cobbled street in an unnamed town and she was watching people as they went about their daily business. Emily said that she worked hard as a cleaning maid in a large house called Beethoven that belonged to a lord and lady, but she couldn't tell me their names.

There was a man in Emily's life, Jonathan, who looked after the horses at the big house. But she told me she did not want to marry Jonathan.

"Marriage causes pain," she said. I asked what made her say that. "The lady of the house is very unhappy because the lord treats her so badly," she explained. "They have three children, aged four, six and seven. The lord is violent and angry and difficult. And he drinks too much."

Emily said she stayed away from him as much as she could. Jonathan lived in a cottage next to the stables and although she felt that Jonathan wanted more from their relationship she was having none of it. For her, it was companionship and fun. Nor did she want children.

"I don't like them, I have no desire for them."

Horses were a different matter, though.

"I like horses and I go with Jonathan sometimes in the carriage." Emily went on to say that she did healing work, both with the horses and with the children of the big house. I asked her to tell me more about that but she seemed reluctant to say too much. She only said that when, for instance, the children had been caned, she would comfort them.

"It's in a way they don't understand. I take away their pain, I take their pain through me." What about her work with horses? "The horses talk to me, they appreciate how Jonathan cares for them. I can heal the horses too, they tell me where they are hurt."

She told me she was able to read and write. When I asked what date this was she didn't know so, as she was in the street, I encouraged her to find a newspaper seller and read me the date on the newspaper. It was Wednesday the 24th September, 1788.

I next met Emily when she was thirty. She was in a field with some horses and two children – her own children! She was still working at the big house although not as much, but she had overcome her doubts and married Jonathan. They had a son Jonathan, known as Little Jonny, and a daughter Emily Rose. The children would play in the field while she rode the horses. She didn't talk to anyone about her healing ability.

"People would think I'm a witch if they knew how I worked with horses… Lots of horses talk to me as I walk down the High Street. I do what I can to help them as I pass."

I invited Emily to move forward to the next important event in her life, and it was certainly dramatic. She was now forty-one and a fire was raging through the thatched roof of her cottage. The children were trapped inside and she and Jonathan were desperately trying to get them out. But they couldn't reach their children, who died in the fire. At this point, Miranda was crying gently on the couch.

"We lost the children." Jonathan did not cope well with the loss and started to drink heavily. "I'm trying to be there for him."

The end of Emily's life came when she was sixty-eight. Jonathan had passed a few years earlier and Emily said she had pneumonia and was very frail. When I asked her to look back over her life she said that, overall, she had been very fortunate and had had her fair share of luck. She had a message for Miranda.

"Believe in your inner magic, don't barrier away love." Emily's passing thought was, "I can now be free."

When I asked the soul to review that life, I was told, "She always wanted more. She so wanted to be her true self, to be free to share her healing. She always felt it was her responsibility to keep the family upbeat, in the big house and in her own home." The goals for this lifetime were to share the healing, to be strong and not to be afraid of success. There would be many challenges, mainly to overcome the pressure of not fitting in, of being different. Miranda would have to, "Be bold, have courage, believe."

All of this made perfect sense to Miranda when she returned from her past life journey. She said that the experience had been intense, especially regarding the fire and the loss of her children. But the interaction with horses had been wonderful too. She was delighted that she had brought Emily's gift into this lifetime and was indeed now free to use it openly, even though many people did not quite understand it.

It was only when I looked at Miranda's notes after the session that I realised she had told me previously that she had a fear of fire. When I next saw her, she said that there had been a complete change in this.

"The intense emotion has gone," she said, "there are no more shudders." She also said that her sleep had improved considerably and that, having processed the experience as Emily, she felt much more confident about moving her business forward.

Veronica was in her mid-fifties when she came to see me. After her business career had come to an end, she'd trained as a homeopath and was passionate about it. However, a combination of serious health issues and troubles within the family meant that she had not been able to work for some time. She was trying to get her life back on track and, being on her own spiritual journey, she felt that exploring a past life could well provide some answers to at least some of the challenges she'd had to face. Once she had settled into a nice deep state of relaxation she was able to find the doorway to the most relevant past life with ease.

We met a girl who gave her name as Margaret – "You can call me Maggie, they all do" – who said she was around fifteen years-old. Maggie told me that she had pink cloth wrapped round her feet and she was wearing a brown dress with a white apron. She explained that she was out in the woods and she was very scared but did not know why. At this point, Veronica had tears running down her cheeks.

"I'm in a clearing in the woods. It's very sunny. I know this place well, I've come here to look for some herbs… I live close to here, in the woods, in a very small place. There's a stove with things on it all the time and a ladder goes up to a platform thing. There's a table there with lots of stuff on it."

Maggie told me that she lived in that little hut with an old woman who found her when she had been abandoned as a baby. The old woman worked with herbs and was teaching Maggie to do the same.

"People come to the old woman and she helps them get better."

I asked then, if the old woman helped people, what was Maggie afraid of?

"Soldiers. They don't like us. There are soldiers on horses, they wear metal chain and helmets that are quite pointy and have plain nosepieces. They don't like us helping people. When they come they take things, chickens sometimes, or things we've made. They frighten me because I never know what they will take next." She described the hut as being made of "a white sort of mud" and that she could smell "all sorts of things... lavender, pots boiling, herbs hanging from the roof... it's terribly cluttered here, very homely really."

But before long, Veronica started crying and was clearly agitated.

"Soldiers, it's soldiers!" said Maggie. "They've set fire to the house! They're smashing everything that won't burn. And they've taken Meg, they're dragging her into the woods, they're going to hang her... I'm outside the burning hut, I'm just standing there, I don't know what to do, I'm so frightened. They're not doing anything to me, just smashing everything around me and laughing. I could hear Meg screaming as they dragged her away and I just stood there."

She said it was early autumn and a nice day when the soldiers just arrived. I let the story unfold in its own time as it was a lot for Maggie to take on board.

"The house is still burning," she continued eventually. "I've got nothing. The soldiers have gone, I'm here alone, I'm all alone... maybe I'll go and find Meg, I should have gone earlier. I'm really scared. Maybe that's what I went to look for earlier, but I know what I'm going to find..."

Veronica shed more tears and then Maggie let out a low moan.

"Oh no, she's just hanging there. I'm kneeling underneath her. I should have come earlier, I wish I had done more to save her..."

I encouraged Maggie to move forward, away from that traumatic episode, and I met her again several years later.

"I'm quite a bit older. I live in the same clearing, in a little shack that I made from sticks and earth, and I have a little stove in the clearing. I live on my own but the soldiers can come back at any time… they come and they laugh."

Maggie paused, then gasped, and Veronica's body visibly stiffened.

"There's a soldier coming now, he's got a long spear… he's laughing at me, he kicks me from his horse so I fall over, I can't do anything, I can't run away… He pushes his spear into my neck and he's calling me horrible names like 'whore', 'dirt', 'witch'… He's disgusting… now he's stabbing my stomach… oh my God, he's pissing all over me and laughing… This is it, my life is ending like this…"

Before she died, I asked Maggie to review her life.

"I was so happy, I loved Meg and she loved me, it was only scary when the soldiers came." Her passing thought was, "I hate him, I hate them all."

The soul agreed that this lifetime had been very happy and full of potential. For Veronica's lifetime, the goals were "to achieve and to contribute" and "to be safe" although it would be "difficult to know who to trust" and there would be "struggles". Interestingly, when I asked what gifts or talents the soul would bring into this new life, the response was, "Insight, seeing the other side. Compassion, which will be abused. And integrity." Veronica must not give up because everything she has done so far is not a waste. She must care for herself, honour herself.

When she returned from what had been an intense past life experience, Veronica put her hand to her neck.

"My neck has always been sensitive," she said. "I don't like anyone touching my neck. I always thought I must have been hung." And she'd had serious issues concerning surgery to her stomach area too.

Yet it was not just the scars of the spear wounds that Veronica carried forward from Maggie, it was her natural affinity with homeopathy too, working with herbs and natural remedies in order to heal others.

CHAPTER 13

History as It Happened

In all the years that I have been working with clients exploring their past lives, I have never come across Nefertiti or Napoleon, Marie Curie or Mozart. None of my clients, it seems, had famous lives or, if they did, those lives were not relevant to the work we were doing at the time. After all, for every one Cleopatra there were a thousand or more slaves, so the odds are stacked against it. On the other hand, if there really is reincarnation then Cleopatra will probably be around somewhere… Perhaps sufficient time and lives have passed for any traces of trauma still to be carried and yet, for someone, it may well be that a visit to Egypt could trigger a memory and a journey of discovery.

One well-documented case study is that of an Englishwoman called Joan Grant who published a novel in 1937 called *Winged Pharaoh*. It told the story of Sekeeta, who became co-ruler of Egypt with her brother when their father the pharaoh died. Sekeeta had an affair with a Minoan sculptor and bore a son called Den who subsequently succeeded her on the throne. Experts in Egyptian history and archaeology praised Joan Grant for her impeccable research and the amount of detail about life in ancient Egypt.

It was only several years later that she confessed the book was not a novel at all but an autobiography, Sekeeta being a previous life. Joan had practised the art of psychometry, or 'reading' an object by holding it and receiving mental impressions related to its history. During one such session in 1936, Joan was given a blue scarab that had been brought back from Egypt. After a few moments of holding it, Joan "changed level" as she called it, and started talking about her life in Egypt.

Her husband Leslie was on hand to take notes of her psychometry session so he recorded as much as he could of what she was saying. This experience seemed to open the doors and was the first of some two hundred sessions, in more controlled situations, conducted by Leslie and Joan where she explored the life of Sekeeta.

The details described in the book proved to be totally true, even though archaeologists and researchers took years to uncover, literally, and verify some of them. Joan was asked how it was that she could remember this past life so clearly and with so much detail. She replied that as part of their special training and initiation, those like Sekeeta had to remember at least ten of their past lives. In order to graduate, the students were shut in a tomb for four days and four nights and, during this time, had to survive seven different challenges or ordeals. That whole experience and the training had clearly been so intense that it was still there waiting to be unlocked in Joan's lifetime.

Joan also remembered many other lifetimes, from a wandering minstrel in Italy to a prostitute in France, from a witch who was burned alive to a Native American girl. Later in this life she married Denys Kelsey, who was one of the early pioneers of hypnotherapy and past life regression. They worked together offering professional therapy support to those suffering from phobias and various illnesses.

Roy Stemman has written about a number of people who claim to have been famous in their previous lives, one example being an American, Donald Norsic, who claims he was Tsar Nicholas II. In this life, Norsic is a very successful businessman in his own right with an enviable lifestyle to match; but his intimate knowledge of the life and death of Nicholas II has convinced many researchers of the veracity of his claim.

As Stemman, who interviewed Norsic himself, says, there are a couple of major obstacles to overcome when considering anyone who claims to have been someone famous. First, there is so much information available in the public domain about famous people that the claimant may well have absorbed details at an unconscious, if not at a conscious, level through reading a book, watching a documentary or even going to an exhibition. Secondly, the claimant may simply be suffering from delusions of grandeur and want to be famous, craving attention.

Another example is Sherrie Lea Laird, a Scottish singer who moved to Canada as a child and who is sure she was Marilyn Monroe. After many years of work with past life regression therapist Dr Adrian Finkelstein, the findings were published in a book called *Marilyn Monroe Returns: The Healing of a Soul.* Then there's Nick Bunick, who was told by separate psychics that he had lived in the time of Jesus, and further research in the form of recorded regressions revealed what seems to be a life as the apostle Paul. Bunick published a book called *Time for Truth* and established a foundation with the same name to 'correct' the distortions of the original message of Paul and Jesus.

Whilst I have not discovered anyone famous in work with clients, I have met some very interesting characters who lived through important chapters of history. Joanna was in her mid-forties when she came to see me. A career woman and single mother, she was always on the go, juggling commitments, priorities and time. Stress and pressure were constant features of her daily life, and personal time for relaxation was almost unknown. She wanted to explore the theme of relationships since she wanted a man in her life yet only seemed to attract destructive partnerships. She also told me that she had a major presentation coming up and that she did not just dislike public speaking, she was scared stiff of it.

By the time we came to do the past life session, Joanna had been into the deep state of relaxation a few times already and enjoyed the fact that the peaceful feeling stayed with her long after the session was over, so she was quite happy to go there again. She quickly found a doorway to go through and there we met a young lady called Nina, who told us that she was in her twenties and that she was wearing a knee-length clingy red dress and furry slippers. It was the 1920s and she was in London.

Nina explained that she was indoors, in a room that had a red swirly carpet, dark wooden furniture and a large window with no curtains. The view was of buildings in the distance and a lamp was lit just outside the window. She seemed confused.

"I'm just standing looking out of the window. I don't know why I'm here. I'm waiting but I don't know what for. I feel I'm in a hotel, I feel guilty but I've done nothing wrong. I'm not relaxed, it's not a good feeling, I don't know what to do next." I asked Nina to tell me more about herself. "I'm not single, but I don't feel married, I feel engaged. There's a ring, diamond and ruby, it's big, it's a family ring." I asked about her family. "Victorian father, nothing else. I can see a pipe and a monocle, and old-fashioned green check clothes. My father is stern, austere. He's well-to-do, quite wealthy… I see books and velvet around my father, an academic maybe, he reads a lot. There's no sense of a mother figure. There's a younger sister, quite a lot younger, babyish. Her name is Rosie."

Having set those parameters, I next met Nina in her forties.

"I'm not engaged any more. I think I'm married but I can't

feel a ring. I'm wearing a dress, it's pink and white and grey, old-fashioned, with a little pattern. I seem to be studying, I'm in a different room, sitting down. There are lots of books."

I encouraged Nina to tell me more about what was going on in her life.

"There's something significant I'm going to achieve, to do with books. It feels like women's votes stuff, feminism. It feels like I'm being a bit naughty, I'm feeling like Emmeline Pankhurst, someone who speaks out a lot on boxes in parks and squares and so on. Sometimes I get into trouble for being outspoken. I'm feeling very much London, politics, I imagine carriages and things. I'm quite well-known, wealthy. I feel I'm not getting much support, I'm out on a limb. I like what I'm doing. I have lots of female friends.

"There's not a strong feeling of a husband, the Dad figure is stronger. He's disapproving. A husband is there, I have a lot in common with him but he's weak. He's separate, wishy-washy, he wears grey. He's nothing to do with my work, he's a banker or something traditional.

"There's trouble with the police, street scenes, pubs, drinking… being a woman in places I shouldn't be in, where it's not acceptable to be. They are quite brawly places but I am feeling excited. I shouldn't be doing it, it's a bit like an underworld. There's lots of red – the colour of the lamps, the room I'm in, red wool, just feelings of red."

Nina moved on to her fifties or sixties, she was not sure which, and I asked her what she was doing.

"I'm doing something significant, I don't know what. There are lots of other people. I'm making an important speech in Parliament. There are more men than women. It's an important cause for me, I don't know what it is. There's lots of green leather and wood and it smells of old men! Whatever I'm supposed to do, it was a success… something for poor people, children, orphans. People are euphoric, they're clapping, hats are being thrown in the air outside."

I let her continue with that part of her life as it was clearly important but she moved herself forward.

"I've accomplished what I needed to accomplish, there's not much left to do. I feel not that happy for some reason, I don't know why. I'm wearing grey, I've given up a bit. Life's a bit drab and boring. I'm not getting much fun out of my life anymore. It's over, I feel a bit forgotten. I was famous and well-known, now I've been forgotten about. It's back to a boring existence. I'm not fighting any more, it's all drab and grey, I don't have a lot of 'get up and go' like I did. I feel quickly older, I feel lonely, side-lined, insignificant, irritated… but I can't be bothered to fight for anything, there's nothing I'm passionate about.

"I don't feel I have family but Rosie my little sister keeps popping up. She's dressed in pink and white and has a cute face. She doesn't get much older. Father is there and a very weak husbandy character. Female friends are making an effort but I'm shutting myself away. I live in a big house but I don't come out much anymore, I haven't got that much energy, not now. The room I am in has big sash windows, a fireplace, lots of separate chairs for different views. I read and write a lot, there are lots of books. It's a big Victorian room with high ceilings. The view I see is trees, lamp posts. It's quite an open space, quite grand. The address is Grosvenor Gardens, number nine."

I met Nina again at the end of her life.

"I'm not old enough to die," she said. "I was knocked down outside. I was crossing the road, I was taken by surprise. I was knocked down by something, a horse rearing perhaps? I don't go out often and when I did, something happened. There was a policeman involved. I'm quite hurt but there's no blood. It was a big shock.

"I'm lying in bed, the doctor is there but there's no-one else around. I'm quite lonely, really. The doctor is looking concerned, there's not a lot he can do, he's just there. I'm living in one bedroom in a big house. My bed, the chairs and so on, they are all in one room. I think I die there. I don't want to die. I wasted the last few years. I regret that. I know I'm going to die. There's nobody else here, I don't know this doctor."

I asked Nina to review the life she led.

"I'm proud. I was lonely at the end. I didn't have children, my passion was whatever I did. I wasn't as caring or soft as I could have been. I was young and passionate in a red dress. Something happened… the cause, the weak man… the young girl in the red dress was more exciting, the streets and the brawling were exciting. The rest was pink and white. My life was amazing, it was written about. I'm not happy being here, I want to go back to the scenes with red in them."

Her passing thought was of "somebody lost in love, red roses, something that didn't quite happen. There's regret. I didn't have this passionate thing for my adult life. I'm dying with no passion in my life, regretting…"

The soul's review of Nina was that she was still the girl in the red dress who never got to do what she wanted to do. The goals for this lifetime were to be happy and healthy, to be a home-owner, secure in a home. The obstacles in the pathway would be "Being intelligent, because it sets you apart from most" and "Anger, seeing red too easily, impatience."

There are some interesting points to note from Nina's account of her life. First, you may have noted that she often said, "it feels like…" or "it seems that…" as though she were detached from the actual situation. Sometimes it can be that a client will experience an entire lifetime from, as it were, an 'observation post': they are looking down on it, like being in a box at the theatre and watching a play unfolding on stage. Certainly, what came across for me was Nina's detachment from aspects of her life, especially those relating to the "husbandy thing", the grey man who was weak and boring. It was perhaps not surprising that there were no children from the marriage.

Nina was in her prime when she was fired up and passionate about her cause: the speech she gave, presumably in the House of

Commons, was about "poor people, children, orphans". Whatever her aim was, she succeeded but then, it seems, there was nothing else left to fight for. She went from the lady in red, feeling the adrenalin rush as she went to places where she should not really have been to being a lady in grey, shutting herself away and distancing herself from family and friends.

Knowing that she had been such a fighter and a campaigner, and a major orator, in that life inspired Joanna. She could understand about attracting men who seemed nice enough but then actually could not keep up with her. They were weak and relied on her to do everything for them, almost like the orphans she was campaigning to help.

I was not able to track down Nina in the history books, but does that matter? Not really, I believe. So was it all a figment of Joanna's imagination? Perhaps, but doubtful. Being a bright lady, she could certainly have picked up some of the basic details of Victorian life during this life. But, as many of the leading therapists in this field have all said, "You can't make up emotions," and the changes in mood from the lady in red to the grey lady were very clear.

Kelly was a very bright, bubbly lady who worked in the armed forces. She came to me because, as she put it, "I need to sort out the whole relationship thing." She had just come out of a relationship of several years; it had been messy and she was still quite emotional about it all.

In that deep state of relaxation, Kelly soon found the door she wanted to go through and there we met Jemima, who told me it was 1858 and she was fifteen years-old. She was wearing black shoes and a blue day dress. Jemima said that she was in the hallway of her home, which was a large house with a sweeping staircase, outside of town. At the back of the house was the cotton plantation that her father owned in Tennessee, USA. She had two brothers, George and James, who were both older than her. George had gone to be a soldier whilst James "doesn't do anything."

Her mother home-educated Jemima so that she could read and write. What about her father?

"I don't see him a lot, he's busy working." Jemima explained that there were, of course, slaves living and working on the plantation but, she insisted, "We do look after them." There were lots of arguments about slavery in the house, it seems, and Jemima didn't quite understand it all. She said that it was much quieter in the house when George wasn't there. He had been gone a year and it would be two more years until he came back for good. He was at military college somewhere on the East Coast, a long way away. According to Jemima, James did not know what he wanted to do. He did not want to be a soldier, which is what his father wanted him to do, but he didn't help with the plantation either. "Daddy's favourite is George," confided Jemima.

Having set the scene, I next met Jemima during a party at her home. She said she was seventeen and wearing a green satin frock. There was a band playing and lots of people dancing. George was there in his army uniform but, as Jemima noticed, "He's not the same anymore, he's more serious than he was." I asked about the rest of the family. "Mummy is in the corner, talking to the people who run the next plantation," Jemima said. "I don't know where Daddy is and I can't see James, I don't know where he's gone, he was here earlier.

"George has brought a friend from army school to stay. He's very nice, his name is Francis, he's not from around here, he's from Pennsylvania… I like dancing, I still don't know where James is… George is not happy that I am talking to Francis, but Francis is nice. He dances with me. Francis doesn't seem to like the way we live, he doesn't like slaves… Mummy says it's time for bed, I'm not allowed to stay up any longer. She doesn't like me talking to Francis either. I don't want to leave the party but I have no choice."

The following day after breakfast, George, Francis and Jemima went riding. It was a lovely warm day and they rested by a lake, George was teasing Jemima in a friendly, brotherly sort of way. Francis told her about Pennsylvania and about his family; he had a brother and a sister the same age as Jemima. George and Francis talked about the scandal from the night before – James had gone to the barn with a girl, nobody would say who the girl was but she lived locally and everyone was talking about it.

A week later, it was time for Francis to leave. Jemima did not want him to go and Francis did not want to leave either. George, seeing how the wind was blowing, told Jemima she should "stick with southern men".

Two years later, in 1862, Jemima was in Washington with Francis who was working there. "Nobody likes me being here," she said, "they don't like southerners in Washington." She had recently got married to Francis and although her family did not approve, his family liked her and they were fine. They rarely got to see Francis' family, though, because he was always working in the War Department.

She said that she did not see James at all. The girl he was with in the barn was from a nearby plantation and was due to marry someone else, so James was packed off to join the army. Jemima's father had died, leaving her mother at home. By rights, George should have inherited the plantation and run it but he was still in the army. He was married and his wife was with his mother at the plantation.

"The war has started," Jemima continued, "and people call me a traitor. It's really hard here in Washington. The South is trying to secede and create their own union. Francis is in the War Department, planning, he's very important, a general I think. We don't have children and I don't see a lot of him nowadays. It's lonely here in Washington."

I next found Jemima in Virginia.

"I'm twenty-two now and I have a little girl coming up two, her name is Lily. We have a house but there's just me and Lily, I have to do everything. Francis is fighting, I haven't seen him in a year and I haven't heard from him in six months.

"I have to entertain men to earn money. I'm disgusted with myself. I've been doing it for the last four months. The men are soldiers, sometimes they can't or won't even pay. They come along, they do what they want and then they leave. Sometimes I have enough money to try and get some food for us. I'm so hungry. The soldiers don't bring food, I have to hide food for Lily, she stays downstairs while I'm with the men upstairs.

"I get up, I find some food for Lily. I have a cow but I have to keep it hidden or the soldiers would take it. I milk the cow, clean the house and try to grow some vegetables in the garden. I used to have chickens but the soldiers took them so we barely have anything now. I don't know if my husband is alive or dead, he doesn't send us any money anymore. I don't know what else to do.

"There's a camp nearby for these southern soldiers. They come in the afternoon, looking for anything to take, then they have their way. They make me have sex with them and sometimes they might pay. They are dirty and smelly, they haven't washed in months. They call me Yankee lover, Yankee sympathiser. I feel alone, miserable, ashamed… I don't want my daughter to grow up like this."

Three years further on, Francis had been home for about three months. Jemima was at home, it was winter time, it was snowing and very cold. Francis was chopping wood.

"He doesn't talk to me, I think he knows." Francis was not injured in the war but he would not talk about what happened to him and he slept in a separate room to Jemima. She said that she was miserable now that Francis was home. "He's only here because of Lily, he dotes on her but barely speaks to me."

The end of Jemima's life came when she was just thirty years-old. Francis had left with Lily, leaving her all alone. She was in a field not far from her home and she was just lying there, waiting to die, hungry and depressed and not wanting to live anymore. Her passing thought was, "What a relief." The soul's review of that life was, "She was alone. The lesson is to be happy in yourself and with yourself. Next time, she must like herself, be happy in herself." The soul said that it found the idea of coming back for another incarnation both daunting and scary.

Although Kelly did not understand the relevance of the American Civil War, she could totally understand the challenges that Jemima faced around relationships. Was it wise, after all, for Jemima to follow her heart and be with Francis? Should she have taken George's advice and stuck with a southerner? If she had stayed at home on the plantation, or married a southerner, she would not have faced the racism in Washington, nor had to put up with the humiliation and sexual abuse from her own kind, southern soldiers. She did what she had to do in order to survive but ultimately it cost her marriage. The abuse and feelings of low esteem and low self-worth echoed with Kelly who said she often felt "used and abused".

Historically, Jemima's facts were correct. The American Civil War started in 1861 and ended in 1865. It was prompted by the election of Abraham Lincoln, a staunch anti-slavery Republican, as President in 1861. Following his election victory, seven southern states – South Carolina, Mississippi, Florida, Alabama, Georgia, Louisiana and Texas – carried out their threat to secede from the Union and form their own Confederation. They were closely followed by Virginia, Arkansas, Tennessee and North Carolina.

It is interesting to note that, after the period in Washington, Jemima had a home in Virginia back in the south, and that's where Francis returned to after the war. The war was very bitter, and it divided loyalties and families, as we saw so clearly through Jemima's eyes.

After a lot of healing work, Kelly felt that her self-esteem and self-confidence had increased. She had a much deeper understanding of how she approached relationships and how this had opened her up to being taken advantage of. The battle, for Kelly at least, had been won.

CHAPTER 14

Physical Issues

It is not uncommon for 'reminders' of physical injuries or wounds to be carried forward from one lifetime to another. Unusual birthmarks, for instance, can often be traced back to an old battle wound or burn. In his book *Other Lives, Other Selves*, Roger Woolger refers to the ground-breaking work done by Morris Netherton, reported in his book *Past Lives Therapy*. The majority of cases here described physical conditions in this lifetime that had their root cause in a past life, including epilepsy, ulcers, migraine and even cancers.

"My own findings," says Woolger, "fully confirm Netherton's pioneer work. A surprising number of physical complaints do indeed have a past life story behind them which, when re-enacted cathartically, can lead to substantial relief and often to quite rapid recovery." He quotes, for example, a woman with eye problems and asthma who remembered a life as a mediaeval monk accused of leading a whole village into heretical beliefs. The monk's punishment was to watch the whole village be burned alive before him, 'his eyes watering and his lungs heaving at the smoke from the burning flesh'.

Monica was a very bright lady in her mid-forties. Originally from Italy, she had now settled in England with her boyfriend and they both had good jobs. When she came to see me, she had a lot of pain in her back and her neck, and indeed wore a brace on her neck to help alleviate the pressure. She'd had a serious car accident twenty years earlier and assumed it was all to do with that.

However, the physiotherapists and osteopaths working with her had said that the problem was not her back or neck but rather her right foot, although they could find nothing physically wrong with it. She was at her wits' end; so when someone suggested she should come to see me, her attitude was one of "Well, there's nothing to lose" rather than real enthusiasm.

She went into the deep state of relaxation and found a past life very easily. We met a woman in her thirties who did not know her name. This woman was completely naked and was clearly confused. I shall call her Carla for now. Carla told me she was in a forest, it was dark, she was alone and she was scared. Why was she there?

"I may have been here a long time on my own, I don't know how I got here... I don't live here, I can't remember my home, I can't remember anything... I'm naked, I'm going to hurt my feet, I can't walk, I'm in the middle of nowhere... I don't know how I got here. It's very strange, I don't have clothes, I don't have shoes."

Rather than taking Carla forward, I took her back to where the story started. At around twenty years-old she was in a nice big, warm house.

"There's a party going on, I'm just watching people... I'm wearing a dress – no, it's a skirt with lots of colours, and a tee-shirt, and flat shoes."

Carla was clearly comfortable at the party and she knew some people there, if not everyone, and was happy to socialise and dip in and out of the various conversations that were going on. The house stood on its own and was near the edge of a forest. She wanted to smoke a cigarette, which was not allowed in the house, so she went outside. She could hear the people at the party laughing and having a good time.

I asked if she was on her own there; perhaps she could have a look around to see whether there was anyone else nearby? She paused.

"Someone came to see me here outside," she went on after a while. "A man, a strange man. His conversation is bizarre, he doesn't talk like the young men do. He's older, I would say around thirty-five. He tells me his name is Roberto and he knows the forest very well, it's a beautiful place. He asks me to go with him for a walk in this beautiful forest. I don't know him but, okay, why not, someone at the party must know him…

"I went with him but suddenly he became very strange, he wanted to get me off the footpath and go somewhere else… I'm twenty, I'm skinny, I'm not strong, I have to go with him… We end up in another wooden house in the forest. He is forcing me to drink something, sleeping pills, water… I have to take them…

"When I wake up, I am tied to a bed, I can't move. That man is telling me he is looking for a wife – me. I'll have to do the cleaning and cooking and look after him. He doesn't want sex but he wants a housekeeper. I don't want to do that, of course I don't want to do that, but what can I do? I'm tied to a bed.

"He's wearing a grey suit and a hat, he must work in a bank, he looks posh, normal, but he's obviously not. He's giving me food, telling me to stay quiet, he'll be back tonight. Then he went out and left me there for the day. When he came home he said if I was nice he would take off the ropes and then I could cook us both a nice meal. What can I do? I have no choice, I can't escape, I don't know what to do. So I cook. He's not aggressive, he's not violent, he doesn't want sex, he just wants me to cook and to clean and do the washing. I have no choice.

"I did that for ten years. I didn't go out at all, I really didn't try, I was much too scared that he would find me and do something bad to me. But one evening he went out and forgot to lock the door. Now

I'm getting out as fast as I can. There's no time to find any shoes, I'm just running, running… it's dark, I'm completely lost. There are so many trees… Oh! I've fallen, I hit a big stone, I've twisted my foot or maybe broken it, I can feel it's bleeding, it's very painful. I can't run anymore, I have to crawl. I'm so scared, I don't know what to do. He mustn't find me. I have been running for so long, there's no road, I'm so scared… I can hear people, I can hear voices, but not his voice. There's a man and a woman… they are camping, they see me, they come to help me, they ask if I am okay. I tell them my story, I haven't seen my family for ten years. These people took me in and gave me water and shelter and somehow got in touch with the police."

Carla was taken to hospital. She had broken her right foot in three places and was told she would never walk properly again. "But," she said, "I'm alive and I am grateful for that." The police came to the hospital and took a statement from her. She was of course able to describe the man and the inside of the wooden cabin but nothing else. She was not able to tell them her name or any other personal details.

The police found the man, though. He had abducted other women in a similar way and the one before Carla had died, he told them, so he needed a replacement. When she left hospital, the State helped her to find a small flat and work that she could do in another small town away from the area so she could start a new life. But she had no memory of her old life at all, apart from the decade spent in the wooden cabin with her captor.

Having followed Carla's story this far, I moved her forward and found her visiting friends for an evening out at a restaurant. She seemed philosophical about the ten years she was captive and the time before.

"I never found those memories, they are gone forever. I'm used to it now, I don't try anymore. If my family has not found me, well, perhaps there's a reason for that. My body is not balanced properly of course, my foot is not working.

PHYSICAL ISSUES

"I am thirty-five now and living on my own. My friends have brought a man with them to the restaurant to meet me. He is nice, I like him. Will something happen? Why not? I am attracted to this man. I asked him out, he accepted, we went to a restaurant. For a long time there was no sex, my foot is not nice, I am very shy about my body, but something has to be done... He invited me to his house for a last drink and I went. Will anything happen? It will not be easy to be naked with him – can he accept me like this or not? We dated several times and finally the moment happened, he was very gentle, there were no problems, it was lovely. I felt alive, like a real woman again, it was as if I'd been dead for all those years."

Carla told me that the nice man, John, was a bus driver. She was in a lot of pain constantly with her foot and she had to take a lot of medication. She said that she felt very low, and so tired of the pain that she could not do very much.

"I sometimes think of suicide, the pain is so bad. I know I've got to live but I don't want to anymore. I am so depressed, I can't take the pain anymore."

I moved Carla to the point of her death when she was just forty years-old.

"I just can't take the pain anymore. There's no cure, I can't see the point, I just want to be out of it all. I'm taking so many pills I will die." Before she passed, I asked Carla to review her life. "It was not a bad life but the consequences of that one decision were terrible. If I look back, I've suffered for so long, I can't remember the nice moments, the pain is overwhelming." Her passing thought was, "It's done, there's no more pain."

It was clear that the injury in that lifetime, breaking her right foot in three places, was still present in Monica's current life. In order to understand a bit more about what was going on, and with Monica still in a deep state of relaxation, I spoke to the right foot, back in the lifetime of Carla. It was sullen, like a sulky teenager!

"What do you want me to say? It was her fault, she didn't take care of me or the rest of her body." I pointed out to the foot that it had caused Carla a lot of pain over many years. "I just wanted revenge because she hurt me," it retorted. And now that Carla had taken her own life, because of the pain you caused her? "I feel stupid because she's dead. There was no point in causing her that pain really, was there?"

So what about the situation that Monica finds herself in now, in this current lifetime?

"Of course this lifetime has to do with that lifetime because, again, she's not taking care of her body. She will probably injure herself again. She is smoking again too… I'm pushing her to take care of herself, to do something positive for her body, like the gym, that's all. She can have a life, she can eat and smoke and all of that, but I need the gym." I pointed out that Monica was in too much pain to consider doing anything like going to the gym right now. "That's right," the foot conceded. "That's silly, it's too much. I should probably stop."

I negotiated a deal with the foot, the neck and the back, in order to bring Monica back into balance. The foot said it would ease off the pain, but insisted that Monica should have a professional trainer or physiotherapist at the gym, or alternatively she could start with some gentle Pilates, one-to-one.

The neck agreed with the deal. It told me that Monica had had a bad chair at home, but had just bought a new one "especially for me". The message from the neck was, "Take care of yourself, lovely body, you have a good nature, take care of you."

The back also supported the deal, saying, "I agree. If she does what she says, I agree to leave her alone. My advice is the same as neck – be nice and gentle with you, you are always hard on yourself. The whole body is not happy with her, especially skin, she does not take care of skin, so we gave her some allergies."

So then I needed to speak to the skin about Monica's allergies.

"I agree," it replied. "When foot, back and neck co-operate, I will co-operate too. She never liked her body, ever since she was a young teenager or maybe even twelve. Foot will talk for the body." And the rest of the body duly agreed to the deal: if Monica started to take better care of herself, to respect her body and to be more gentle on herself, the body would ensure that everything would be alright!

When Monica was fully awake again, we discussed the deal I had negotiated with the various parts of the body. She commented it was interesting that the skin had said she had not liked her body since the age of twelve, confirming that it was "absolutely right".

A couple of months later I received an email from her. She told me that the pains in her foot had indeed reduced and that she felt much more in balance. She had taken heed of the warnings from her body and was making positive steps to be kinder to herself and not 'beat herself up'.

Daniel was a young man in his late twenties who had, by his own admission, lost his way. "I need a complete re-boot," was how he put it. He always wanted more than he had and felt envious of what others had, even though there was nothing wrong with all that he owned. He had completely lost a sense of direction and perspective.

Going into a past life, a man called Sa'id introduced himself. He was thirty-eight years-old and was wearing sandals, a light cotton robe and a turban wrap-style headdress. I did not specifically ask for a year, but my intuition told me we had travelled back millennia to find this particular lifetime. Setting the scene, Sa'id told me that he was in the countryside and there were hills in the distance. He was a goat farmer and had four goats. It was springtime, everything was starting to go green, so the goats were happy. He told me he could smell pine, it was cold and fresh, early morning.

He told me that he lived in a mud hut with a thatched roof. I asked about his family and this is where the story started to unfold.

"I did have a family. They were murdered by a rival farmer's gang. I stole his flock of goats. He retaliated, took everything – my house, my farm, my family, all my goats, everything was destroyed, my wife and my boy aged four. I stole his flock because I had nothing and he had everything. He took his goats back and more. He is a man to be feared. But he had the best livestock and I wanted some to increase my flock."

How did Sa'id feel about this situation?

"It makes me feel angry. I let them down, I was a bad example for my boy. Now I feel… well, I don't feel, I just wander, I'm lost. I just look after my goats and that's that."

A few years later, the man whose goats he stole, the local gang leader called Akbar, caught up with him. Akbar's henchmen came for him, kidnapped him and brought him to a hut, tying him to a chair. Akbar was waiting for him.

"He wants to torture me, to teach me a lesson. I'm going to have to work for him now… I won't work for him… He's got a blade, he's waving it around close to my throat… He's torn out all my fingernails… he's threatening to cut off my ear… I've got to work for him. I hate it, he's a monster, I wish he'd just kill me. It's really hot… he's got a brand to brand me on my chest… I can't breathe."

At this point, Daniel's chest lifted off the couch and he winced in pain. His forehead was perspiring.

"He's done this so everyone knows what I've done, who I am, I belong to him now… I have no other identity any more. They untie me, they throw me out of the hut. It's bright, I can't see… desert, dry, hot.

"He killed my goats. They were all I had left. I feel broken, alone, I feel like a fool, I did this to myself. I was arrogant and naïve. I thought I could take on the world and now I've got nothing. The goats, they were my last companions."

Five years later, Sa'id was one of Akbar's henchmen and had been sent on a mission to burn down the hut of an old man who owed Akbar money.

"I'm in a hut again, a different hut, it's night-time. The hut is on fire, it smells of smoke and ashes and fumes. I'm covered in soot, I'm black. I set the hut on fire, on Akbar's orders. The old man is frail and weak, he's a farmer. There's wheat in the hut, a few cooking utensils, nothing else. He didn't pay, he owes Akbar money, he's owed the money for a long time so he knew this was coming. The old man has a family, he said he hasn't seen them for a while, his wife and his daughter and a grandson.

"I want to feel sorry for him but I feel nothing. I've forgotten what it's like to have someone to care about. Burning his hut makes me feel angry at myself. I wish I had the ability to give a damn about him but I don't. I don't care about anything anymore, I just take each day as it comes.

"Is Akbar pleased with me? I wouldn't go that far, I'm a means to an end. He doesn't treat anyone well, he's a savage brute, he's not human, he's the devil in human form.

"I burned the man's hut. I hit the man because he talked back to me. The building's starting to collapse and I've got to get out, I'm making for the door. A beam falls down, it lands on my hand… it's so heavy, I can't lift it up. I'm shouting for help. The old man's knocked out, there's someone outside because Akbar never lets us work alone but he won't help, he won't risk his life for me. I wouldn't do it for him. It's getting smoky, I can't breathe… there's no air. I can't lift this beam… there are flames everywhere… nobody is helping me."

At this point Daniel was moving around on the couch, clearly in great discomfort.

"I got my hand free but I'm trapped by the fire. I'm in a corner, there's no way out. I'm just accepting it, this is it for me. My hand is useless, it's shattered. I wouldn't be able to lift the beam to get out… It's so smoky."

At the point of death, I asked Sa'id to review his life.

"I have an overwhelming sense of regret. I should have… I could have done more, been a better role model, I sure as hell shouldn't have worked for that prick. I wish I'd done it differently."

The soul's review of that lifetime was, as one would expect, insightful. It told me that there was much to learn from that life, saying, "He should have thought about the consequences of his actions. He should have thought before he acted. Even though it wasn't the right thing, he was trying to do all he could for his family. He should have taken the long way and not tried to take the short-cut."

Daniel was clearly shaken by this experience; whatever he might have been expecting, it certainly wasn't that! We went through the salient points of Sa'id's story. He'd had a family, a wife and a son, and a few goats, presumably enough to survive on and scrape a living from. But he wanted more. Instead of planning how to increase his herd, he stole more goats. And not just from anyone, but from the equivalent of the local Mafia boss! That was naïve and the consequences were brutal and far-reaching.

In our first session Daniel had admitted that he felt guilty about not being close to family and friends. He also felt guilty because he recognised that he was selfish, not looking at the consequences of his actions, not caring about that. And he didn't do things for other people unless there was a personal gain.

Naturally, I asked Daniel after the session if he'd ever had any issues with his chest or with his breathing. He said that he frequently felt a tightness across his chest, which could well link to the branding with a hot iron. He also reminded me that he'd had asthma since childhood and still used an inhaler – an echo, perhaps, of the smoke in the old man's hut and him suffocating to death. He had also admitted to having a phobia, "Anything to do with fingernails or toenails." Sa'id had his fingernails ripped out by the boss.

Daniel reported later that the regression had given him much to think about, and the issues around his chest and his breathing had both improved markedly.

CHAPTER 15

Money and Sex

Humans learned early in their evolution that money and sex have several things in common: they can both bring considerable pleasure or considerable pain, they can both be used in a healthy, positive way or in a toxic, unhealthy way, and they can both be used for personal gain and manipulation of others!

One of the interesting things to remember when we are considering our own past lives is that we have all been the bad guys (or girls) as well as the good ones. We have quite possibly all been murderers or rapists, thieves or vagabonds, the abuser or the abused, the perpetrator or the victim. The fact that we have evolved to where we find ourselves today shows that we have learned from those experiences, perhaps working out some karma along the way, and made choices to move forward in more positive, loving pathways.

It is so important not to judge anyone because we cannot know what journey their soul is on. It may be, for example, that a perpetrator and a victim may be members of the same soul group, each helping the other to learn valuable lessons or to balance karma. It was Shri Babaji Haidakhan who said, in one of his blessings, "There is no saint without a past and no sinner without a future."

It is perhaps not surprising, therefore, that the issues of sexual abuse and money are at the end of quite a few threads that we unravel from this current lifetime, leading to one long ago and far away.

When I worked in Portugal, people would sometimes come to me wanting a session of past life regression 'just for fun', and I would always read them the 'terms and conditions' of undergoing the process.

"It may be curiosity and a bit of fun for you," I would say, "but your unconscious, your higher self, has pulled the strings that have brought you here right now. There is something that needs to be resolved and this session may well do that. So be prepared for some surprises, or some insights, that you were not expecting!"

One such client was Maria, a Portuguese lady in her late forties who worked for an English company there. Her English was excellent and she was a friend of the lady who owned the clinic in Lisbon that I worked at.

"I have heard a lot about regression and I'm curious to know more," she said. "I do meditation, I consider myself a spiritual person, and I would love to know who I was before." Again, I cautioned Maria.

"Just because you are spiritual in this life, does not mean that you were spiritual in all of your previous lives."

Because of her meditation practice, Maria slid gently into a very deep state of relaxation and easily found the door into a past life. We met Balvit, an Indian man in his fifties who told me that, although he was Indian by birth, he was in Egypt. He had travelled there with his mother many years before and they had settled in a small town. Balvit was an ambitious man, motivated by power and money, and he became a tax collector. He wanted to show me his mark of office, a slim, ornate wooden pole about a metre long; it was beautifully painted, he pointed out, and had some kind of ribbons or tassels at its top end.

"Everyone knows that I am a tax collector when they see my stick," he explained. "They know I am a very important man, very powerful."

I asked Balvit where he was and what he was doing, and Maria let out a big sigh, almost a groan.

"I am in the marketplace," Balvit replied. "Today was market day, and one of my duties is to collect the taxes for the stalls from the people who come to the market to sell their wares." There didn't seem to be any issue with that until he continued, "My mother is now old, she cannot work as she once did, so she sells vegetables at the market. Today she did not sell many vegetables and so she didn't have enough money to pay the tax for the stall." There was a pause before Balvit went on.

"The punishment for not paying the tax is a beating with my stick." Here Maria's hand rose as though Balvit were waving his stick. "I am an important man, a powerful man, I could not let my mother get away with not paying her tax, so I beat her." Another long pause.

"But I beat her too hard and she died."

I asked Balvit how he felt about that.

"It was my job," he retorted, in an arrogant sort of tone. "She knew that she had to pay the tax and she didn't pay. I am the tax collector, I had a job to do, so I beat her. I was only doing my job."

"But you beat her too much, didn't you?" I suggested.

And then the façade of bravado broke. Maria started sobbing, big heaving sobs, tears rolling down her cheeks. It was a few minutes until the sobbing subsided and Maria's breathing returned to a more gentle rhythm.

"I killed my own mother," Balvit said quietly. "I beat my own mother to death and now I am cursed." I let him sit with that realisation for a few minutes and then asked how he felt now. "All I ever wanted was money and power," he told me. "That's why I brought my mother to Egypt, that's why I became a tax collector. I loved the power, the status. I was an important man, I had lots of money… and now look what I have done. I have killed my own mother for the sake of a few paltry coins. I could have paid that out of the money I have in my pouch… just a few stupid coins." The full impact of what had happened was now sinking in.

"I loved my mother, I just never told her that. I brought her to Egypt so that she could have a better life too, and she did. But I did not look after her as I should have done. I was not a good son. And now I have killed her. How can she ever forgive me?"

I could almost imagine Balvit there in the marketplace, hanging his head in shame and despair as a crowd gathered. Gone was the swagger and the arrogance of the powerful tax collector and here was the guilt and grief of a desolate son looking at his mother's lifeless body. At the end of his life, Balvit was a broken man.

"I had money, I had status, I had power," he told me, "but nobody liked me, everyone hated me. I was all alone except for my mother and I killed her."

I felt it was important to resolve the issue with his mother before he died in that lifetime, and took him through a process of connecting with the soul of his mother so that there could be closure and, more importantly, forgiveness. That was very emotional and there were more tears, but it became clear that Balvit had indeed been forgiven by his mother and that, at a soul level, all was well, he could die in peace, which is what happened.

I brought Maria back from that intense past life experience and wondered how she would react, bearing in mind that this was meant to be a session for curiosity, 'just for fun'. Once she had composed herself, the very first thing she said was amazing.

"That explains it! My mother lives with my husband and me. She and I get on fine most of the time, but we are always arguing about money and it has been getting worse over the past couple of months."

A few weeks after the session I received an email from her to thank me for the experience. She explained that she had not told her mother anything about the session but that, somehow, strangely, since that date the relationship with her mother had shifted and they no long picked fights over money. "We haven't argued once," Maria said.

What was most interesting about this was that Maria had not come to me with a specific issue to be resolved. She hadn't said anything about the arguments with her mother and I didn't know about her family situation. Yet, at some level, it was time for this issue to be resolved. Moreover, we did not have to go all the way through Balvit's life: we were taken straight to the key point in his life where the trauma happened. That indicates to me that it was Maria's unconscious, or higher self, taking charge of the situation and highlighting where the healing was needed.

Annie was in her mid-thirties when she came to see me, a hard-working single mother who was devoted to her child but struggling with a number of personal issues. Comfort eating was a default setting, but there was also a cocktail of emotions around her child's father and her relationship with him.

We had had a few sessions before the regression, to prepare for it and make sure Annie was comfortable with the process. We found a young woman called Mary who was barefoot, standing on moss. She was wearing a rough brown dress – "like a bag of oats" – and a white pinafore. Mary told me she was quite young and that she felt quite carefree out in the fresh air with the warm springtime sunshine on her face. But something was not quite right.

"I feel sad," she said. "It's not going to last, me feeling so happy, I know it." I asked Mary what she could see around her and she replied that there was an old mansion house. "It feels scary. It's big and old and dark." She told me she lived and worked there too. "I don't like being there, I like being outside. I'm not often allowed outside.

"I have a really awful kind of sexual feeling, like I'm completely controlled and abused in that place... I have images of being held down and sexual acts being performed on me... A man, he's much higher up the system than me, he pins me down, he hits me. He's wearing a red velvet jacket with a waistcoat and a necktie and breeches and black shoes. He's the master. I'm on a long table. He lifts up my skirt and he takes me, he does what he wants. When he's finished, he just walks away. There's nobody else in the room this time. I feel sad and I feel angry but what can I do? This has happened before and there have been others in the room, other men.

"When he's finished I just sit there and cry. Eventually I get up and leave and go to a dark corner. There's a bed thing on the cold, cobbled floor, I curl up with a blanket and I cry. Then someone shouts at me to get back to work. It's like I'm in a kitchen, I see a cauldron in a big fireplace. I make things in the kitchen, I can see flour and bread or something."

I asked about the sexual abuse. Had it been going on a long time? When was the last time?

"Yes, it's been going on a long time, I don't remember how long. Last time was not long ago. Even though I don't really like it at the time, it makes me feel special that he's chosen me. I think I love him."

I next met Mary when she was in her twenties.

"He did it again but he went in... behind. There were lots of them. The man is older and fatter now. My hands are tied. They whipped me. I was wearing a dress, they ripped it at the back and they ripped off my underclothes... The men are there drinking and laughing, I've seen them here before..." Annie, lying on the couch, gave a big sigh before Mary continued. "It hurts when he takes me. He's done it before but not like this, like he's angry. Then they all do it, there are seven of them... I don't say anything, they're all laughing as they go...

"Someone comes and helps me, they cut my wrists free and help me get to somewhere safe, then they just sit and hold me. They are two young women my sort of age. One of them is called Bess, it feels very safe to be held by her, I like her very much... But I feel like we're ripped apart, she's sent away."

Five years later, Mary was in a very different place. She was wearing a white blouse, jodhpurs and shiny black boots, and she was grooming horses. She told me she was not at the old manor house but living with her brother where she felt safe and loved. I asked how she found her brother.

"I had to leave the manor house, it was either that or die. And so I walked and walked until I found my brother. He's a vicar at St Andrew's. He's married, he has a wife and some children... I look after myself. I work in a mill, crushing things and carrying things, I ride the cart."

Mary gave the year as 1842 but said she was not sure, and said she thought it was King James on the throne but again she was not sure. At the end of her life Mary was no longer living with her brother. She was in her kitchen in front of the fire and told me that she was very sick with an infection.

"I'm very weak," she said, "and I'm going to die soon. It feels peaceful, I want to die. My life was hard, I want to forget it. I did get married, I have a husband. I've got long, black curly hair, and I'm wearing a white nightgown right up to my neck." Mary was happy to go and her passing thought was simply, "Goodbye."

The soul's review of that lifetime was that it was very hard work, tiring, and she worked her fingers to the bone. The goals for this lifetime were quite simple.

"I'd like to be happy, to be loved, to have children and animals. I want contentment and peace and understanding. I don't want hassle. I don't really want to be wealthy, just enough is fine. I want food.

183

There wasn't food, we couldn't grow it, it wasn't there, there was never enough food." The challenges that the soul set itself were 'resistance to people' and 'just wanting food'. When asked what the feeling was about this present lifetime, the soul said, "It's not working. There's so much oppression, I can't find a way through it, it makes me want to give up. This feels the most difficult life yet…"

The abuse that Mary suffered was horrific but, if the stories told by my clients are anything to go by, it was not at all uncommon. Mary's confusion was curious – we might say nowadays it was naïvety – thinking that she was somehow special because the master chose to repeatedly rape her, and even believing she might be in love with him. But then over the years she saw the situation for what it really was and plucked up the courage to walk away.

I can only speak from my professional experience, but this blurring of emotions is not uncommon, even when the abuse has gone on for a long time. "He loves me really," is something I have heard many, many times, from women who also tell me of physical, mental and emotional abuse. At whatever level, abuse wears down the self-confidence of the victim and leads them to doubt their own thought processes, their own reason, until they are completely at the mercy of the perpetrator.

Abuse has no place in a relationship that is built on mutual love, respect and understanding. How interesting that in this lifetime Annie once again has relationship issues with variations on the same themes. And the food issue has returned as well. In Mary's life it was because of starvation, there was never enough food, and in this lifetime it is the comfort blanket, the reassurance.

Work with Annie continued until she got a new job and moved away from the area. By that time her relationship with food was much healthier and she had understood far more about the dynamics of the various relationships in her life, especially where sex and control were concerned.

MONEY AND SEX

Lara was a glamourous lady who came to me with an unusual request: she had lost her libido and wanted me to find it for her! She explained that she and her husband had been happily married for some years and the physical side of the relationship was important for both of them. But over the last couple of years it had slowed down and lately there had been no sex at all. Lara emphasised that other areas of the relationship were fine, there were no obvious stress points; jobs and finances were stable, there were no children to worry about, no issues around alcohol or drugs and no major arguments.

So where to look for Lara's missing libido? I always work with a pendulum close by on the desk and, if in doubt, I use it to ask for advice. It clearly indicated that the answer would be found in a past life, and I have long since learned not to argue with the pendulum!

Although Lara had not done any work of this kind before she came to see me, she was a natural and by the time we got to this past life session she easily went into a deep state of relaxation. She found the door into the past life that her unconscious, her higher self, had guided her to, and there we met Claudette. Claudette told me she was around twenty years-old and that she was wearing a white above-the-knee summer dress and no shoes. It was a beautiful day outside, Claudette said, but she was inside at a hotel somewhere, looking out of the window. She was on her own, and seemed quite vague when I asked what she was doing there.

"I feel like a little girl lost, very insecure." She explained that she was staying indoors to be protected from something or someone outside. "There is danger for me outside. I don't know what, maybe just a feeling…" A couple of hours later, Claudette was still inside the hotel, refusing to go out, even though she told me that people were enjoying lunch in the garden. I tried to discover the nature of this danger that lurked outside and asked whether it was because of who she was. "It could be," she said.

She eventually ventured outside to what was a family gathering, a celebration of something, with lots of people there.

"I don't want to be involved with the family. I am here because I have to be but I am not enjoying it… I am looking at the people but I am not being with them. I know them but I don't want to be there."

There was a pause. I could see that Lara was processing all this so there was no rush.

"There's a man I don't want to see," Claudette continued. "I can't see his face… he is maybe an uncle. He is close family but he is not my father. I don't like the way he is looking at me… Everyone is happy and smiling. He is too, but not me. I am unhappy about all of this. Something is happening with that man. He's not the person he shows. Nobody can see it but I can see it because I have the feeling he's doing bad things to me… This is a lovely place, there is a terrace, the sun… This is not a good moment for me at all. He's drinking, drinking, drinking. It's his birthday, he's the star of the show."

We moved on to later at the party.

"I'm still there, outside of everyone, just observing. Someone is asking me to join in and have a drink. I want to keep control of the situation of that man who keeps looking at me… He's coming to see me to ask me to join in. He takes my waist, I push him away. He says, 'You're just a little girl,' and laughs. He goes back to the party, to his show… He's disgusting, he has big fingers…"

I asked Claudette to tell me about the first time she'd had those emotions about that man, and she went back to when she just seven years-old.

"I have long hair and a long fringe. I'm in a nightdress, it's long and white… I am in my bed, that man is coming. He's coming in the bed with me, under the cover with me… he's starting to put his tongue out… he's pulling my nightdress up, he's putting his tongue everywhere, my breast, my tummy… he's putting his fingers in my special place down there… it's disgusting. Why is he doing that? What is that? Nothing is said, nothing at all. Now he's stopping, he's going. He didn't stay very long, he didn't say anything, just put his fingers to his lips. 'Shhh.' He did bad things.

"I hate him. I would like to tell everyone what he did but I can't because he's in the family, nobody would believe me… He had sex with me very regularly over the years, he puts his fingers in me, I feel excited, I'm twelve years-old now… He is excited too, of course. I don't try to avoid it, really. I am enjoying it, I am touching him too…

"He tells me he loves me. I tell him I love him, but as an uncle, it doesn't mean anything… It happened a lot, we had an affair. I was sixteen when I understood that it wasn't normal. I stopped the affair. I told him if he continued I would tell everyone, but I wouldn't say anything if he stopped. That was four years ago and now I am at his birthday party…"

I asked Claudette if she had other boyfriends away from that affair.

"Yes, I do have boyfriends but we always split up. Sex doesn't mean anything to me. I don't know what love is because of what that man did to me. I'm completely lost. I don't know what is right, who I can have sex with or not… my body doesn't know what to feel and when to feel it… I'm not scared of that man, I quite like him. He's never been violent with me, he just likes little girls. He's about thirty years older than me."

I took Claudette back to the party and asked what was going on there.

"It's late lunchtime, a beautiful day with blue sky and sunshine. The party finishes in the evening… Everyone is leaving… It seems I live at that hotel, I don't want to live at home anymore. My parents should have done more, they should have protected me… That man doesn't bother me now."

The next time I met Claudette was on her wedding day and she was waiting for the ceremony to get under way. I asked her to describe her wedding dress.

"It's long and very full, not complicated. It's white and silky, with long sleeves. I have a long veil. I don't have any flowers and I

187

don't have any jewellery, nothing. My husband's name is Stefan, I can't remember his family name. We are getting married in a small church, it's summer, the 17th July. I can't remember the year."

I asked Claudette to talk me through the day, how she was feeling, how the day unfolded and so on.

"I am not really enjoying the day. I am getting married but it won't change anything. I am still lost when it comes to sex and love. He wanted to get married, I said yes. He's about my age, thirty-five, a very nice guy. He's a bit lost with me because I am a strong character, independent, and he doesn't know how to handle me… I'm not really in love with him. I think he's a lawyer, there's money… I've had sex with him, of course, I started having sex early, it's what I learned. My husband knows I don't want children, he has known that from the beginning. I don't want to put my children in the same situation that I was in, I don't want them suffering… maybe he wants children, but he doesn't say anything."

At the end of her life, Claudette was around seventy years-old and still married to Stefan, who had by then retired, and they were living a quiet life.

"I am almost at the end of my life and I am happy it's going to be the end of my life. I have not been happy in my life at all, I feel broken. I've had pleasant moments but I have not had a happy life. No children. The marriage was all right, he was a good husband, he took care of me. I never told him about that man… He died, my uncle, I didn't go to the funeral…"

Reviewing her life, Claudette said, "I am at home. I feel very tired, I'm just really old, I feel I'm going to die. I'm glad this life will be finished. It was a boring life." Her passing thought was, "So that's it, no more."

The soul's review of that life was insightful.

"It was a sad life. She was broken so young, there were no reference points. She had a very strong personality. She was a nice person, but lost with men, and she suffered because of it." The only goal that the soul set for this lifetime was to enjoy life without feeling guilty about anything. There were just two challenges: to be happy with a boyfriend, wanting to get married and enjoy the rest of her life with him, and to find the perfect job.

Soon after that session, Lara had to have surgery and we agreed that she would get back to me when she felt ready. Two months passed and then I got an email, out of the blue.

"I think I never told you that my libido is back! It's not as I knew it but it's a more normal libido than it was. I'm very happy about it. You've been very good, thank you."

Sadly, it is still true today that the majority of sexual abuse inflicted on young children is carried out by people they know and trust. As we saw with Claudette, that can stay with them throughout their lives. The abuse started when Claudette was still very much a child, just seven years-old. By the time she was twelve and probably going through puberty with hormones all over the place, she admitted that she was enjoying the sexual encounters with an experienced older man.

But that was mixed with guilt and confusion since he was her uncle, after all. As she said, it was only when she was sixteen that she realised it wasn't normal and by then she had been in an abusive sexual relationship for almost a decade. No wonder her relationships were confusing, both for her and, probably, for her boyfriends too. Although she got married and settled down in that lifetime, Claudette never really found peace of mind, haunted by the trauma of her childhood that tainted the whole of her life. No wonder it made such an impression on the soul that it was carried forward.

In this lifetime, Lara had a happy marriage although interestingly, as before, she did not want children. What was it that triggered the memory of that past life, that turned off the libido? We talked about that and concluded that it may well have been a holiday taken a couple of years earlier at a hotel that resembled the one seen in the past life. There had even been a big party in the gardens while they were there, which may have added to the memory.

What really mattered to me was that the session proved yet again that the real root cause of an issue in this lifetime, however strange it may seem, is very often in a past life.

CHAPTER 16

The Spiritual

Over the years I have been asked many questions about the whole field of past life regression. I can only respond from my own experiences and from the research that I have done, although often I will refer people to books written by people such as Dr Ian Stevenson, Dr Brian Weiss, Roger Woolger, Michael Newton, Dolores Cannon and so on. They each have their own approach to past life work and yet they all agree on the main point, there is life before life.

One of the most common questions put to me is whether animals have a soul, closely followed by, "Do people have other lives as animals?"

In order to address those questions we need to look at the more spiritual aspects of life and of the soul. My firm belief, confirmed by my own research and the work I have done over so many years with my clients, is that the soul is eternal. When it comes into a physical incarnation, it 'puts on an overcoat' and takes on an identity as whatever or whoever it may be for that lifetime. Then at the end of that life, the soul takes off the overcoat, leaves it behind and goes back to that non-physical state, the life-between-lives world.

You will know from what I have shared in this book that, in my work with clients, I follow the soul to that life-between-lives place and bring it to the point of preparing the script for this current lifetime. Thus my client is reminded of the goals, challenges and advice for this particular incarnation and able to support the healing process. There are those, such as the renowned Michael Newton, whose work focuses primarily on that life-between-lives, going into much more depth on that soul-level work.

Well, do animals have souls? They are living, sentient creatures as we are. We have all seen for ourselves in our own homes or in television programmes how they care for their young, look after the weak of the tribe and mourn their dead. They have personality and character, they display emotions from joy to grief. It would seem reasonable to assume, therefore, that, yes, they do have souls. And there are many mediums who will connect with and 'bring through' their client's deceased pet, describing it accurately and highlighting some characteristics, even passing on 'messages'.[22] Eastern philosophies such as Hinduism and Buddhism certainly believe that all creatures have souls, which is why they treat them so differently to mainly Western cultures, where that belief does not exist.

Can animals reincarnate as people, then, or people as animals? In the literature, there are two answers to this – yes and no – and both sides seem totally convinced that they are right!

Sri Chinmoy, an internationally-respected spiritual leader from India, wrote in his book *Death and Reincarnation*, that 'In the march of evolution, once we have accepted the human life, we do not go back to the animal kingdom…'[23] And elsewhere he added, 'The soul does not go back to animal condition, but a part of the vital personality may disjoin itself and join an animal birth to work out its animal propensities there. But the soul, the psychic being, once

---

[22] See *Furry Spirits* by Glynis Amy Allen, published by Local Legend
[23] Aum Publications, U.S. (1989)

having reached the human consciousness, cannot go back to the inferior animal consciousness any more than it can go back into a tree or an ephemeral insect.'

On the other hand, His Eminence Tsem Tulku Rinpoche, a world-renowned Buddhist teacher, said that, 'Animals can become human again and vice-versa after death. We take repetitive rebirths due to karma, instinct, imprint and ego. When we hold on to a strong sense of ego we generate karma. Karma from actions of body, speech and mind propel us to endlessly take rebirth in myriads of places in order to continue to satisfy the ego.' You can see already that the question is quickly spiralling into a major philosophical debate, and we have not mentioned consciousness yet.

I have only personally come across a few cases where the client appears to remember a past life as something other than a human. I phrase it like that because those clients tended to be highly-evolved souls who have also had lives on other planets – which is another entirely different topic! This next short story, from a very spiritual young lady, is not a deep dive into the detail but gives an idea of how the session went.

Shannon was in her thirties and newly married when she came to see me. She worked with animals as a teacher and a trainer, and wanted to explore a past life to see whether it could shed light on any of the issues on her 'shopping list' of being emotionally "all over the place", constantly worrying about money, and having a fear of heights.

She took very little encouragement to go into a deep state of relaxation and from there we were off on a journey into the unknown… First, we met a young woman who told me she was on the edge of some woods, looking at a grassy clearing. It was summertime, she was wearing a summer dress and flowery sandals. She was there alone and she thought she might have run away, just for fun. I asked where she had run away from.

"Base camp," she said. "There are treehouses and tepees and wooden structures… about thirty people in all live there."

The girl told me that her father was a hunter and her mother looked after the children, quite a few of them by the sound of it. She said that the weather was the same all year round at that place, which she felt was a different planet to this one. She thought it was called Azuria but she was not sure. She confirmed that there were other communities on the planet like the one that she lived in, and that they were all human in form although shorter than the average human.

Moving on through the girl's life, it became clear that this planet was struck by meteors and all inhabitants were killed. From there, the soul found itself floating out there in the universe, full of joy. However, down here on planet Earth, the clock was ticking so I asked the soul to move on to its next incarnation and it duly did.

"I'm a dolphin. I'm a dolphin," it said, still full of joy. We explored that for a short while and then I asked, "How many incarnations have you had between that life as a dolphin and this current one?" Back came the answer, "I've had eighteen others in between."

I asked whether Shannon's nagging concern about money came from a past life.

"Yes, there have been lives when she was very poor. There was one during the Fire of London. She was a very poor child, she had nothing, she didn't live a very long time in that one either."

I asked where Shannon's fear of heights originated.

"The general fear is accumulated over time. The fear of heights comes from a life when she nearly fell from a very high place. It was somewhere mountainous, she was just a child."

The soul was clearly quite happy to answer my questions, so I asked what form it had taken in the incarnation immediately before this present one.

"I was an animal, a tiger. Yes, a tiger."

The question had to be raised, so I suggested, "Some people would say that it is not possible for a soul to change between animal and human form…" The answer came back straight away, in a very definite tone of voice.

"Well, they're wrong, aren't they? We can change between animals and humans, and so on." Had Shannon worked with horses before, as she did in the present lifetime? "Yes, she lived with horses."

Fascinating as that conversation was, it could have gone on for hours and time was against us, so I had to bring Shannon back to the present. Once she was grounded, I asked for her feedback.

"I've not been very good at being alive," she laughed. "I've been like a lemming!" But she said she really felt like a dolphin, with a sense of complete freedom in the ocean and a different sort of knowing and wisdom. And as for the horses? "I did live with horses," she said. "I saw myself as a Native American Indian looking after the wild horses on the plains."

The information gleaned from this session, far more than is given here, put many aspects of her life into perspective; and the understanding of the root cause of her concerns about money and fear of heights put those to rest too. The healing and deep soul connection work that was done proved very beneficial for Shannon as she set off on the journey of married life.

Some will say that Shannon made it all up, that it was all in her imagination. What a load of rubbish. Others may say, "Thank goodness, I thought I was the only one."

Well, for me it's all about the healing. Being a spiritual woman, perhaps an 'old soul' who'd had many lives, it didn't surprise me that she'd had at least one on another planet; although having been both a dolphin and a tiger did raise even my eyebrow. What was more important was that it provided answers for her, it resolved multiple issues and, as she said later, "Things just fell into place and settled down."

There can sometimes be a very spiritual overtone to a past life journey, as was the case with Joy, an early-fifties lady who worked as a healer.

She said that she had two teenage sons and had a strong sense that one of them had been with her before in a past life. That in itself is not at all unusual. Family members are frequently part of the same soul group, although the roles can change: mother and son can become husband and wife, or master and slave, or teacher and pupil, for example. It all depends on which dynamic would work most effectively in order for those concerned to learn their life lessons.

Joy's son Timothy was highly sensitive. He had been bullied at school for being 'different' and had been reprimanded by a teacher for not talking in class (how unusual is that!). She explained that he was psychic, he picked up all sorts of things about people and, as youngsters do, did not realise that not everyone else could do that because it was so natural for him. He struggled to make friends, and desperately wanted to be 'normal'. A highly intelligent child, he had ongoing issues with authority at his school where he did not feel sufficiently stretched or challenged.

"Why do I even have to bother with talking?" he had said one day when he came home. "Where I come from, we don't need language, it's all done telepathically."

Luckily for Timothy – or had he chosen his mother well? – Joy took on board what he said and did not make a big fuss about it as he was only about eight years-old at the time.

"But," she told me, "I've kept an eye on him since then and I just know that he is different. He could well be one of those from another place."

This opens up another debate about whether there is life on other planets and, if so, what are they doing here in human form? As yet, we do not have any real answer although, looking at information sources away from the mainstream, we find what seems to be a wealth of 'evidence' to support that theory.

As to why they are in human form, well, at a soul level, presumably they want to have a human experience. There are those who say that some of the off-world races do not have the same wide, subtle range of emotions that humans do and this is something that attracts their attention. Others believe that our planet itself is going through a massive energetic shift, bringing in these other souls, almost like going on holiday to somewhere completely different to experience the place, the culture and the people (if on a much larger scale!).

I have mentioned the internationally respected researcher and hypnotherapist Dolores Cannon, who talked about the 'Three Waves of Volunteers' that she identified from her work with clients. Some of these volunteer souls had never lived in a physical body before, whilst others lived as off-world beings in extra-terrestrial civilisations on other planets or had come from other dimensions. All wanted to be on Earth at this time to help humanity 'raise its frequency' through the process of ascension to new energies.

However, because all souls, wherever they are from, pass through what is called the 'veil of forgetfulness' when they incarnate, these off-world volunteers do not remember where they came from or why they are here. It would therefore be very challenging for them to adjust to a world in turmoil with so much disturbed energy in the collective atmosphere. As we see from Joy's story, life here on bumpy old planet Earth can be anything but easy for them.

Our session had a strong spiritual overlays and Joy's spirit guides were apparently with her all the way through.

"I'm being protected from making the same mistakes I've made before," she said, "but I don't think I can do this… I feel as though I'm being forced, it's not entirely my choice to come here again… my soul group wanted to come here and so I agreed. I felt strong with them but now I feel so alone, there's nobody from my group here."

I asked Joy's higher self, her unconscious mind, whether Joy really was alone in this incarnation.

"No," was the response, and two people close to Joy were named.

"But I felt I needed everybody," Joy said, "and a lot of them are not here... Until I find them, I don't feel safe, I could lose myself again."

"They are all here," her higher self replied. "They have all incarnated, you are not alone."

Joy, in a deep state of relaxation, made some movements on the couch as though settling down to business. Then she paused, sighed deeply, and the story started to unfold.

"I'm in the middle of a semicircle, there is blackness between me and them, loneliness, I can't see them... it's my fault we can't connect... they are all waiting there, nobody else has the blackness." At this point, Joy covered her head with the light blanket that was laid over her. "I want to go and hide, I feel so undeserving, they're stuck with me..." There was a pause and I just held the space as Joy gathered herself and processed what was happening until she was ready to move on. "They're creating a web, like a spider's web... there is no more darkness... I feel emotional, they feel happy. This is my family, but not my blood family... these others are supporting my blood family.

"Timothy is there, pointing in a certain direction, and he's saying, 'We need to be there.' There's a sense of urgency. I've got to show the way, I'm the leader of the squadron—" here she laughs "—I'm in the middle, I've got to show the way..."

Then she said that Timothy grabbed her and they were both looking at planet Earth, where the souls of some close family members who had died were forming a cloud and moving away, letting in more light. They were told that one in particular would incarnate as a Native American shaman.

I asked to be told more about Timothy's role and Joy told me what she was seeing.

"Timothy is standing in the place of the Wise One, addressing the whole group. He is animated, he is proposing what needs to be done. I don't need to lead anymore now, I can take a back seat...

He looks really big, we're all looking up to him and he is okay with that. He is saying, 'Alignment, be aligned with each other. Continue to create that web, the web is extending to other places and other dimensions.' We have to put that web into the ground, it is not ready to be used yet but the Earth needs it… He needs me to play my part.

"I know I have to stop right in front of him, we are the masculine and feminine energies needed to ground the web with the use of an ankh. I'm doing it in front of Timothy. I feel like a learner in front of a teacher… am I doing it right? He's amused, he knows I know how to do it… The ankh is going into the soil now, I move so the others can see it… We are anchoring the network into Mother Earth, anchoring these spots for whoever needs them into the centre of the Earth. People can step on them and they will be grounded into the power points." There was another long pause as she processed all this safely.

"This is helping people to get grounded. I've got to sit on one of the power points here because I am being realigned. Timothy is in front of me, his right hand is on my head, he is smiling… Everyone is starting to hold hands, it's part of the impact of the ankh keys that have been planted, people are sharing that connection as well as grounding.

"Now my attention is drawn behind us, I see my other son Thomas, it's rather dark behind him. I'm concerned but Timothy is not. Thomas is being approached by beings of light, the darkness around him is being changed to orange… he needed help too. He is sitting at the back of the group… he has very long, strange arms and he is acting as a shield, protecting us." At this point, Joy, on the couch, raised her knees and shifted on the couch.

"I'm standing up again, I'm moving around, the job is done. Everyone else is standing up now too, they are all very happy, they are relaxed. We are not going to be attacked again… Timothy is just standing and smiling, enjoying what he is seeing. He knows there is a lot ahead, we are not out of the woods yet."

It became clear, as Joy visibly relaxed and stretched out, that the work was done. I brought her back from that deep state of relaxation and when she was fully grounded I asked for her feedback. She told me she had experienced lots of period-type pains in her abdomen at points during the session, but apart from that it all made a lot of sense to her, especially the relationship with Timothy in that 'other place' and an understanding of the work they had done. It was a powerful session and one that was both insightful and reassuring to Joy.

Postscript

There is nothing new about the concept of reincarnation, as we have seen, although it is only relatively recently that, in the West in particular, there has been an understanding of the role that past life regression can play in healing issues in this current lifetime.

The soul, I believe, is eternal and carries the sum total of all the experiences, from joyous to tragic, across all of its incarnations. This is what makes us the unique individuals that we are. For more than twenty-five years I have supported ordinary men and woman on journeys to find the past lives that hold keys to issues holding them back in their lives. What they found has often been traumatic and sometimes surprising, yet the resulting release of old 'stuff' has consistently shown how effective the healing process is.

As more research is done by those applying rigorous methodology, and as more case studies come to light that can be checked and verified beyond reasonable doubt, my hope is that there will be a wider acceptance of the process. This may in turn encourage more people to look to this as a route for resolving whatever troubles are preventing them from being the very best that they can be.

If you are interested in exploring past life regression for healing, my suggestion would be to read a few of the books referred to here, as they will give you a feel for the different approaches.

- ❖ Check a therapist's credentials: he or she should belong to at least one professional body.

- ❖ Check their website: does what you see and read resonate with you?
- ❖ Contact them, talk by phone or on a video call. Get a feeling for who they are, their character. Are they caring?
- ❖ Ask them questions. Only if and when you are comfortable should you go to the next stage, a personal face-to-face session.

It is a fascinating experience, a true voyage of discovery, and I feel sure that you will come out of it with important insights and a better understanding of who you really are. Moreover, hopefully, you will experience healing.

If you have enjoyed this book…

Local Legend is committed to publishing the very best spiritual writing, both fiction and non-fiction. You may also enjoy:

SPINACH SOUP FOR THE WALLS
Lynne Harkes (ISBN 978-1-907203-46-6)

This is a message of hope for anyone in despair and a call to see our troubles as opportunities for growth. Lynne had a privileged life in wonderful and colourful places, from South America to Africa, and she tells us of the magnificent natural world there and the resilience of its people. Yet she found herself retreating into isolation and unhappiness, out of touch with spirituality. This is the story of how she learned to "recognise the remarkable in the ordinary", rediscovering herself and a new way of being.

Winner of a Gold Medal in the
national *Wishing Shelf Book Awards*.

"…a spiritually rewarding book… Highly recommended."

FURRY SPIRITS
Glynis Amy Allen (ISBN 978-1-910027-48-6)

The loss of a pet can be devastating. They have been members of our family, unconditionally loving and much more than 'a furry friend'. We need to know whether they live on and can perhaps communicate with us. This wonderful page-turning book, by a bestselling author and hereditary medium, has the answers and much more. In everyday language and often with humour, Glynis gives fascinating and evidential stories of animal survival as well as describing the amazing healing and psychic abilities of animals.

GHOSTS OF THE NHS
Glynis Amy Allen (ISBN 978-1-910027-34-9)

It is rare to find an account of interaction with the spirit world that is so wonderfully down-to-earth! The author simply gives us one extraordinary true story after another, as entertaining as they are evidential. Glynis worked for thirty years as a senior hospital nurse in the National Health Service, mostly in A&E wards. Almost on a daily basis, she would see patients' souls leave their bodies escorted by spirit relatives or find herself working alongside spirit doctors – not to mention the Grey Lady, a frequent ethereal visitor! A unique contribution to our understanding of life, this book was an immediate bestseller.

Winner of the SILVER MEDAL in the
national *Wishing Shelf Awards*.

"What a fascinating read. The author has a way of putting across a story that is compelling and honest… highly recommended!"

AURA CHILD
A I Kaymen (ISBN 978-1-907203-71-8)

One of the most astonishing books ever written, telling the true story of a genuine Indigo child. Genevieve grew up in a normal London family but from an early age realised that she had very special spiritual and psychic gifts. She saw the energy fields around living things, read people's thoughts and even found herself slipping through time and able to converse with the spirits of those who had lived in her neighbourhood. This is an uplifting and inspiring book for what it tells us about the nature of our minds.

THE QUIRKY MEDIUM
Alison Wynne-Ryder (ISBN 978-1-907203-47-3)

Alison is the co-host of the TV show *Rescue Mediums*, in which she puts herself in real danger to free homes of lost and often malicious spirits. Yet she is a most reluctant medium, afraid of ghosts! This is her amazing and often very funny autobiography, taking us back stage of the television production as well as describing how she came to discover the psychic gifts that have brought her an international following.

Winner of the Silver Medal in the national *Wishing Shelf Book Awards*.

"Almost impossible to put down."

SPIRIT SHOWS THE WAY
Pam Brittan (ISBN 978-1-910027-28-8)

A clairvoyant medium for over thirty years and highly respected throughout the UK, Pam describes herself as "an ordinary woman with an extraordinary gift." Despite many personal difficulties, she has shared this gift tirelessly and brought comfort and understanding of the Spirit to a great many people. Here, she inspires us to realise our own innate gifts and to trust that Spirit will always guide us on the right path.

5P1R1T R3V3L4T10N5
Nigel Peace (ISBN 978-1-907203-14-5)

With descriptions of more than a hundred proven prophetic dreams and many more everyday synchronicities, the author shows us that, without doubt, we can know the future and that everyone can receive genuine spiritual guidance for our lives' challenges. World-renowned biologist Dr Rupert Sheldrake has endorsed this book as "…vivid and fascinating… pioneering research…"

A national runner-up in *The People's Book Prize* awards.

A MESSAGE FROM SOURCE
Grace Gabriella Puskas (ISBN 978-1-910027-00-4)

Beautiful and inspiring poetry of the Spirit that reaches deep within the consciousness, awakening the reader to higher states of awareness, spiritual connection and love. The author, in familiar and thoughtful language, explores the power of meditation, the nature of the universe and of time, our place within the environment and who we truly are as creative beings of light and sound.

Winner of the Local Legend
national *Spiritual Writing Competition*.

THE HOUSE OF BEING
Peter Walker (ISBN 978-1-910027-26-4)

Acutely observed verse by a master of his craft, showing us the mind, the body and the soul of what it is to be human in this glorious natural world. A linguist and a priest, the author takes us deep beneath the surface of life and writes with sensitivity, compassion and often with searing wit and self-deprecation. This is a collection the reader will return to again and again.

A winner of our national
Spiritual Writing Competition.

ODD DAYS OF HEAVEN
Sandra Bray (ISBN 978-1-910027-17-2)

If you feel that you've lost the joy in your life and are not sure where you're going, this book is written for you. Sandra knows those feelings all too well. Rocked by mid-life events, she refused to be a 'victim' of circumstances and instead resolved to treat them as opportunities for change and growth. She looked for a spiritual 'guidebook' to offer her new thoughts and activities for each day, but couldn't find one – so she wrote it! In this book, and her sequel *Even More Days of Heaven*, we find hundreds of brilliantly researched suggestions, sure to life our spirits.

Runner-up in the Local Legend
national *Spiritual Writing Competition*.

Local Legend titles are available as paperbacks and eBooks. Further details and extracts of these and many other beautiful books for the Mind, Body and Spirit may be seen at

www.local-legend.co.uk